# HOW TO TELL A
# STORY

## THE SECRETS
## OF WRITING
## CAPTIVATING TALES

Peter Rubie

*and*

Gary Provost

**WRITER'S DIGEST BOOKS**
CINCINNATI, OHIO

To Alice, a good friend and
fellow survivor of the "trenches."

This hardcover edition of *How to Tell a Story: The Secrets of Writing Captivating
Tales* features a "self-jacket" that eliminates the need for a separate dust jacket. It
provides sturdy protection for your book while it saves paper, trees and energy.

Other fine Writer's Digest Books are available from your local bookstore or direct
from the publisher.

02   01   00   99   98      5   4   3   2   1

**Library of Congress Cataloging-in-Publication Data**

Rubie, Peter.
   How to tell a story: the secrets of writing captivating tales / by Peter Rubie &
Gary Provost.—1st ed.
     p.    cm.
   Includes index.
   ISBN 0-89879-809-4 (pbk.: alk. paper)
   1. Authorship.   I. Provost, Gary.   II. Title.
PN145.R73   1998
808'.02—dc21
                                                   98-11454
                                                    CIP

Edited by Jack Heffron and Roseann Biederman
Production edited by Marilyn Daiker
Designed by Mary Barnes Clark

# ACKNOWLEDGMENTS

Susan Rabiner, a brilliant editor, for all her help and advice.

My editors, Jack Heffron and Roseann Biederman, for their patience, professionalism, guidance and encouragement.

Gail Provost, whose invaluable help in writing this book improved it 1,000 percent.

Carol Docherty, for her help with the chapter on conflict.

Frank Strunk, a fellow "strummer."

And to Lance and the many Writers Retreat Workshop students and friends of Gary Provost whose active participation in the hothouse of past WRWs was so instrumental in helping to focus and develop this material.

From Gary and me, thank you.
We couldn't have done it without you.

# ABOUT THE AUTHORS

For over two decades, Peter Rubie has been a writer, editor and teacher and is currently a partner in Perkins, Rabiner, Rubie & Associates, Literary Agents.

Before becoming a literary agent, Rubie was fiction editor at Walker and Company in New York City. He is the author of two nonfiction books, *Hispanics in Hollywood* (Garland Press) and *The Elements of Storytelling* (John Wiley), and two novels, *Werewolf* (Longmeadow Press) and *Mindbender* (Lynx Books).

Rubie regularly lectures and writes about the craft of writing fiction for magazines, universities and professional seminars.

He lives in New York City.

Until his untimely death in 1995 at the age of fifty, Gary Provost was arguably the leading teacher of writing in the United States.

He had published thousands of articles and dozens of books, including, most recently, Stephen Bogart's biography of his father, actor Humphrey Bogart (Dutton), and a new mystery series with Berkeley (the first one, *Baffled in Boston*, came out in late 1995). Just before he succumbed to a heart attack, Provost had been contracted to write Kelsey Grammer's biography, *So Far . . .* (Dutton).

Provost was also a contributing editor and regular columnist for *Writer's Digest* magazine and the director of the Writer's Retreat Workshop and Write It/Sell It seminars. He won the National Jewish Book Award for children's fiction and was nominated for a Newbery Medal.

# TABLE OF CONTENTS

# FOREWORD

Gary Provost, one of the great teachers of creative writing in the United States, was in the process of turning his notes and lectures on story sense into a book when he died unexpectedly at the age of fifty. Knowing that he and I were not only friends but shared similar philosophies and ideas about teaching writing, his wife, Gail, and agent, Jeff Herman, asked me to write what is, alas, Gary's last book.

As a result, *How to Tell a Story*, inevitably, is not all in Gary's voice, nor does it contain ideas that are exclusively his. Instead, it is a synthesis of our ideas and is in part the product of many conversations we shared about writing fiction.

Gary was a writer of deceptively simple and crystalline prose and a gifted, empathic teacher with an understanding not only of the process of writing, but of the psychology of the novice writer. His death has left us all the poorer. However, we have his books and his tapes, and we should be thankful that at least this shadow of his excellence can still be shared both by those of us who knew him and those who did not who may still benefit from his legacy.

# INTRODUCTION

What is it about some books that makes them compelling—un-put-downable?

You know the ones I mean: that novel you decided you'd start just before going to sleep and ended up finishing at 6:00 the next morning just when you had to get up for work.

A friend told me (rather irately) of the first night of a much needed vacation with her husband in a French hotel. He wanted to read the new book by a best-selling author so badly that, rather than keep her awake with the reading light on, he spent all night with the book in the bathroom.

What we wouldn't give as writers to be able to have that hold over our readers.

So why is it that one person can tell you about his flight from an erupting volcano and bore you to death, while someone else can tell you why she had to do the same laundry three times last Thursday and have you hanging on every word? How is it that two people can tell the same joke and one of them has you rolling in the aisles while the other makes you squirm in your seat? The answer is the storyteller's grasp of dramatic structure and its role in unleashing the story's emotional power.

Almost every time my friend Gary Provost and I got together and talked about teaching writing, the conversation would eventually get around to whether it was possible to teach students this sense of dramatic structure, or "story sense."

We would discuss why it was that students can write well and yet *what* they write is boring. It gradually became apparent to us that understanding how language works and putting words on the page is not enough.

There is a second equally important element to the writer's craft that is rarely talked about and rarely written about: an awareness of how to structure material in the most effective way to put across the narrative, that has little to do with the ability to use words well. A writer can be way ahead in ability in one skill and way behind in the other.

The reason that I, and 95 percent of all the other people in the industry, stay in publishing when there are better paying jobs elsewhere is that publishing is a compulsive and obsessive career with which to become involved. In short, we do what we do because we love it passionately and because the vast majority of our colleagues, be they editors, agents, or published writers, are brilliant, witty, interesting people whose company is fun.

But our love affair is not specifically with books; that is just the outer form. It is with what publishing is, at its heart: a marketplace for ideas.

I still get a shiver when I stop to consider that I make my living in a marketplace where the best ideas, especially those with the most emotional impact, are powerful and compelling enough that they are eagerly bought and sold. It is a heady thought. We live in a society where, despite its ills and negative elements, we still have enough regard for the product of our best thinkers that we consider their ideas commodities that have definable monetary as well as intellectual value.

This is why a good idea, whether at the heart of a piece of fiction or nonfiction, can sell when it's not that well written; and material that is wonderfully written will not always sell, because at its heart the idea contained within it is overly familiar or mundane, with little emotional impact.

In other words, authors whose books sell have a better developed story sense than their unsuccessful competitors. How do you, the novice writer, improve your chances of getting published? The answer is simple: Make sure your idea is told properly—that is, structured to be the most effective presentation of that idea, at its most emotionally gripping.

## DEFINING STORY SENSE

Story sense is about structure. And the key to effective structure in fiction and narrative nonfiction can be reduced to the writer's ability to create strong, potent characters.

What we mean by this, in short, are characters who are active not passive; characters who are not afraid of conflict; conflict that continues to rise until the narrative's end; writing that is not episodic; story development that is not afraid of playing it big; an appropriate and effective sense of mystery; and opposition to the hero that is formidable enough that it defines and reshapes the hero for the better by story's end without being insurmountable.

Fixing structural problems is what editors and agents do most when fine-tuning the work of the authors with whom they collaborate. So what is it they know that many writers don't?

Soon after I signed the contract to write this book, I was cornered at a party by a successful writer friend with an un-flinching laserlike perception, who asked me: "So how is this book going to be different from the ones you and Gary have written before?" (And implicitly, other books about writing that are already on the shelves.)

While I knew the answer, there I was, drink in hand, suddenly grasping for words to form a succinct answer. Kathy's question haunted me for weeks. All nonfiction books should pose a question, and provide an answer before you start writing them.

What is more important than any "rules" or "dos and don'ts" about writing, what all writers need to keep as keen as a knife blade, is a highly developed sense of dramatic structure—in other words, story sense. The important problems writers must solve are not just *what the story is*, but *how it should be most effectively told.*

Without the ability to understand the difference, you can write *words* brilliantly and still not ever get published.

A quick example: The movie *The Fugitive* is, at its heart, a familiar story with just enough of a modern twist to make it interesting: Executives of a large pharmaceutical company fake data on an ineffective new pill and try to get rid of the one man who can blow the whistle on their fraud, potentially costing them billions of dollars in profits.

The way the story is told, however, is brilliant; and because more and more of our emotional capital becomes invested in the two main characters, played by Harrison Ford and Tommy Lee Jones, the story grips us with a mounting emotional power as it reaches its climax.

## COMPELLING WRITING

Story sense is about honing your instinct for what is both dramatically appealing and dramatically successful. This is something of a mouthful, I know, but it boils down to this: Compelling writing means involving the reader completely in your narrative. That means finding the best way to tell your story, be it fiction or narrative nonfiction; you must learn how to discover and unleash the emotional power of your narrative.

What interests readers is not so much *what* happens, but *who* things happen to. If they don't care about the characters, readers are not really interested in the outcome of the characters' lives, and a reader certainly won't spend the night sitting in a bathtub in a hotel in Paris engrossed in a writer's world while his spouse is asleep in a comfortable bed in the next room.

Writing is a compulsive thing, and what separates those who want to write from those who actually are writers is simply this: Writers write, in some form or another, every day. Just to spend time *thinking* about writing (without thinking specifically about a particular project or problem) and waiting for the muse to pass by is not writing.

To achieve any level of publishable excellence as writers, we must learn to hone our instincts for what works dramatically. The best way to do this is to practice writing and *read, read, read*.

## A GOOD QUERY

Put a group of experienced journalists or writers of fiction in a room, feed them a bunch of ideas for stories, and almost invariably the good ones will pick the *same idea* and want to do something with it.

For example: "Dear Sir, I've written a detective story about a PI in LA in the 1940s in the tradition of Raymond Chandler. . . . " Ho hum. Read it, been there, got the T-shirt. It's been done already—by Raymond Chandler among others.

However: "Dear Sir, What if the seventeenth-century English playwright and spy Christopher Marlowe was forced, by circumstances, to become a private eye to save a friend from the executioner's axe? . . ." Now I'm curious. It's potentially fresh and interesting, though you have to know a lot about England of that period to make it convincing.

In publishing, an industry largely defined by the idiosyncratic taste of editors and agents, *everyone* "gets" a good idea the first time she hears it or sees it. It is the basis for that much hyped and grossly overused Hollywood catchall: the "high-concept idea."

A high-concept idea is one that can be summed up in a sentence or a phrase, and yet has within it enough charisma and excitement that the idea alone provokes an audience to want to read more about it, see how it is developed. The major weakness of high-concept ideas is that too often the summation of the idea is more beguiling than its final development. In other words, the author falls short of the demands of the idea and fails to deliver.

The high-concept idea should be, ideally, an indication of a story's fierceness of focus. Thus it's not always just an onerous marketing burden forced on writers in order to get themselves published. It can be a useful tool for marketing a book that has a clear focus and deals with an interesting and relevant idea, or juxtaposition of ideas. The final developed version of the idea doesn't have to be trite and obvious. Instead, it can be complex and highly literate, and in general these are qualities most editors and agents seek in contemporary fiction and nonfiction. But the central idea of the book or screenplay should be intriguing and focused firmly enough that it is relatively easily summed up.

Here are some examples of successful high-concept ideas:

- A bored housewife meets a visiting photographer, and almost in spite of themselves, they have an affair that rekindles the passions of their youth (*The Bridges of Madison County*, Robert Waller).
- A horse healer meets up with a crippled horse and its crippled rider and attempts to heal both (*The Horse Whisperer*, Nick Evans).
- A young lawyer straight out of law school gets his dream job and then discovers he has sold his soul to the devil and must find a way to get it back (*The Firm*, John Grisham).

In publishing today, what everyone's looking for, in fiction in particular, is a well-written high-concept idea. Analyze almost all published books by previously unknown writers who have "made it" (that is, been published regularly and well), particularly those who hit the best-seller lists, and nine times out of ten, what they have in common is that they are fresh, high-concept ideas. We'll talk more about this in chapter three, "Hooks."

## DEVELOPING STORY SENSE

So how do you learn this mystical storytelling talent? What makes one aspiring novelist or writer of narrative nonfiction more likely to succeed than another? How do you pick out a great idea for a story from the hundreds of other story ideas you get? And then how do you develop it to its best dramatic shape? *In an increasingly tough publishing market, how do you get that edge that will get you published and keep you getting published?*

This book will answer these and other questions.

*How to Tell a Story* is about the dramatic forces that make a story work and how best to unleash the emotional power of your narrative. It is about what creates excitement for the reader, why the reader will get involved with the story and feel *compelled* to turn the page.

You can know all there is to know about style, description,

viewpoint, etc., but without a way to hook them all together, in other words, without a sense of structure or story sense, your grasp of these elements will be limited. Story sense is about understanding drama and dramatic structure—what actors and stand-up comedians call "timing."

The aim of this book is to help you recognize and develop a great idea and then turn it into a compelling narrative that will make even jaded publishing professionals sit up and get excited.

## THE RABBIT KNOWS . . .

When Gary graduated from high school, instead of going to college he hitchhiked around the country from city to city, slept on park benches, panhandled in the parks. And around the time he was twenty, he decided he would write the Great American Novel. It was called *The Rabbit Knows*, and he wrote about five chapters. Not surprisingly, it was about a young man who hitchhiked around the country from city to city, slept on park benches, and panhandled in the parks.

He once confessed to me: "Thankfully I've forgotten almost everything about this book, except for this one sentence: 'He was not quite as salubrious as he might have been on such a day, and so he stood torpidly beside the corroded asphalt-pebbled border of the highway making nugatory conjectures, and his thumb sought some sort of concession to his distress.' "

Gary and I used to joke that may be the worst sentence he ever wrote. I confess that as a junior reporter on a local weekly newspaper, at about the same age as Gary, I wrote a few sentences that were probably worse—and were printed with my byline on them by my editor, no doubt to teach me a lesson for some now-forgotten journalistic transgression.

I don't know whether you've ever written a sentence that bad, but the point is, both Gary and I wrote that awful way once, yet, since then, we have both made a living from writing—selling books, magazine articles, short stories, columns and so forth. So it's reasonable to assume that from the time

Gary and I were writing phrases such as "nugatory conjectures" to now, we learned how to write well.

Pretty obvious thing to say, I suppose.

A lot of writers give up because they believe the ability to write is somehow "in the genes," that you either "have it" (whatever "it" happens to be) or you don't.

But writing and storytelling aren't like that. They are crafts, something you must learn to do effectively. And once you get a firm grasp of the craft, you start to see possibilities and get inspiration, and *that's* where the *art* of storytelling and writing springs from.

## HOW TO TELL A GOOD STORY

Developing story sense is really nothing more than learning to find the most interesting way to tell a good story. So, you ask, "What do you mean by 'a good story'?" That's a good question.

A good story takes readers where they haven't been before in the company of interesting people they learn to care about who are forced to deal with adversity. It is, therefore, best when it is specific about time, place, and task, particularly when it involves unfamiliar and unusual places and activities. The best ideas and the best writing are always simple and direct. You have to learn to trust your instincts and your judgment and listen to the guiding voice they provide. You learn this by practicing and mastering your craft.

Don't feel that after you read the material in this book once you should know everything there is to know about writing. What may seem obvious when we point it out is not so obvious when you are in the middle of writing your story. Read this book over and over. Think of it as a toolbox, and the techniques as tools to help you become a better writer. You're reading this book because you want to learn how to write great stories that will sell, because you are trying to get on paper an idea that won't let go of you and insists that it's a story that should be told to others.

There are many ways to write, and whatever works for you

is how you should proceed. Gary was able to analyze the writing process like few others, and yet, as much as this book may seem to be a lot of rules and jargon, he was the first one to point out to students that writing "isn't a religion." What Gary and I have figured out over many years of hard trial and error *does* work, and it has taken us from prose of the "nugatory conjectures" variety to satisfying careers in writing and publishing. Paying attention to the "tools" we've come up with to discuss writing narrative prose will steer you in the right direction.

As you read about the various aspects of storytelling, it will help a lot if you have a particular story in mind that you want to write. You might also find it helpful to jot down notes on the various elements discussed in this book and apply them to the book you're working on. Keep those notes, along with any exercises you do, in a notebook. After you've written part of your book, or your first draft, go back and read through this material again.

When I studied music, even though I was a guitar player, I was lucky enough to study jazz improvisation with Warne Marsh, one of the great tenor saxophonists. When I first arrived in New York City, he helped me get an apartment. The landlord asked me, in Marsh's company, "Are you a jazz musician, too?" I felt like a fraud saying yes, considering the company I was keeping, and stuttered and hesitated not knowing how to answer when Marsh jumped in and said, somewhat impatiently, "Of course you are." It felt like a weight had been lifted from me, because in truth I realized it is the seriousness of your approach to what you do that defines what you are, not whether or not you made a living at it. I *was* a jazz musician, and I played and practiced music eight to ten hours a day, seven days a week and performed in public as often as I could. I just wasn't in the same class as my teacher. Big difference.

I remember Gary telling a similar story: "When I was a teenager I used to read the writers' magazines. And whenever I used to take these magazines into someplace public, a diner, whatever, I would always put the magazine face down on the counter. The reason was that I was embarrassed about the fact that I was studying writing, embarrassed that people might see that I thought I was a writer. I guess I felt like a fraud. I thought that since I hadn't published anything I had no right to call myself a writer."

## TO BE A WRITER, WRITE!

Perhaps you feel this way? It's worth remembering it isn't what we publish that makes us writers, it's that we *write*. If you write regularly, you can call yourself a writer. It's OK. Think of writing as something like martial arts. There are grades of belt, from white to black, that define your experience. And when you reach black belt, there are grades that define degrees of expertise even among the masters of the craft.

Writing is a profession, like the law or medicine. You don't learn to be a neurosurgeon in three months or six months and then dive in with a scalpel hacking away at people's brains. You put in a lot of time, learning slowly by doing the work over and over. Similarly, writing and storytelling are crafts that develop over time and with practice and take more time to learn than it seems they should.

That feeling Gary and I had of being a fraud is, I guess, somewhat universal. Some time ago, political cartoonist and satirist Jules Feiffer wrote the following, which may strike a chord with you:

> I felt like a fraud, so I learned to fly an airplane. At fifty-thousand feet, I thought "A fraud is flying an airplane." So, I crossed the Atlantic in a rowboat. I docked at Cherborgen. I thought, "A fraud has crossed the Atlantic in a rowboat," so I took a space shot to the moon. On the way home I thought, "A fraud has circled the moon." So, I took a full-page ad in the newspaper and I confessed to the world that I was a fraud. I read the ad and I thought, "A fraud is pretending to be honest."

Perhaps he anticipated some of the feelings you have about

writing. We hope this book will make you feel more like a writer.

Many people believe that story sense is the one thing that can't be taught, that it is only a God-given talent. Neither Gary nor I believe that, or we wouldn't bother to teach or write books like these. After all, we learned it. You can, too.

One final point: *How to Tell a Story* is about writing character-based narratives, whether they are novels; nonfiction accounts, such as true crime or biography; screenplays; plays; etc. The techniques discussed here can be adapted to apply to nonfiction—for example, rethinking the concept of defining a protagonist by how formidable the antagonist is into defining the strength of a nonfiction idea by including the strongest arguments against it in the book—but scholarly or nonnarrative nonfiction is a different topic with a different set of demands made on the writer and is beyond the scope of this book.

*Chapter One*

# Ideas

Getting an idea for a story is not nearly as difficult as it seems. After you've been writing for a while, ideas come to you pretty easily. You may not believe this at the moment, but once you work at developing story ideas, they'll start tumbling out of you, and you must be willing to throw all but the best ones away.

The problem is not getting the idea—it's (1) figuring out a good idea that will sell vs. a weak or mediocre one that won't, and (2) figuring out whether this idea is best written as a book, a short story, a screenplay, a magazine article or what have you.

Once you start developing your "idea muscle," you'll have so many ideas, believe it or not, that writing can become quite frustrating because you'll realize you can't possibly develop them all. So how do you decide which ones to work on?

## A NOTE FOR THE SECOND-TIME NOVELIST

For most of this book, I'm going to assume you haven't published any book-length material yet. However, I'd like to address a brief note to those who might be struggling with their *second* books. For some, first books are relatively easy. They had great ideas and mastered enough technique that, with the help of agents and editors, they got themselves published. But now they have to repeat the trick!

When you're starting out as a writer, and particularly if you've published one book and are now thinking about your second, coming up with a good idea for the next book can seem a Herculean task tinged with a vague air of desperation. That first successful book (that got you published!) was like a nagging child tugging at your clothes, filled with emotion, an idea that came to you and wouldn't go away until you paid it some attention and helped it grow to some sort of maturity.

Before you got published, you thought getting published for the first time would be the biggest obstacle you'd have to face in your writing career. After that it would be all smooth sailing. But now what? Your agent and your editor expect you to come up with something new, at least as good as, if not better than, your first book. If you're not careful, panic can set in, and not far behind that, depression. It seems like you're back where you started. Where will you get this next great idea?

## "WHAT IF . . . ," OR, "SUPPOSE . . ."

An idea is all the things you think about in the creation of your story before the story has plot elements. The idea can be a memory from childhood or a character based on your Aunt Sophie; it might be a gimmick, such as the detective figuring out who committed the murder by pressing the redial button on the phone and finding out who the victim called just before she died. It might be one of these things or a combination of them.

So how do you come up with ideas in the first place?

In the absence of a compelling idea that won't let go, you grope around looking for something to start work on. You watch TV, read newspapers, listen to the radio, eavesdrop on other people's conversations, start asking yourself, What if that happened this way instead?

That seems like a good place. Let's start with, "What if . . . ?" or, "Suppose . . . ?"

What if an advice columnist were murdered? What if the newspaper replaced her by running a contest? These were some of the questions Gary started asking himself when he began to write his murder mystery *Baffled in Boston*. The idea for that came about, incidently, because Gary entered a contest to replace the famous advice columnist Ann Landers, who was retiring. He didn't write about that experience, but he did draw upon it.

What if a policeman tracking down a serial killer in the Blitz of London comes to think the killer is a werewolf? This was the starting idea for my novel *Werewolf.*

Back in the 1800s, there were stories of sea monsters in the North Atlantic. Sailors would come back and report seeing them, and the "monsters" became all the talk. Herman Melville heard these stories and asked himself, What if one of these monsters was a great white whale? What's more, what if his worst enemy was the obsessed captain of a whaling ship? And he wrote *Moby Dick.*

Over in Europe, Jules Verne was listening to the same stories. He asked himself, What if one of these monsters was a submarine? And he wrote *20,000 Leagues Under the Sea.*

H.G. Wells asked himself, What if a man could travel in time? And he sat down and wrote *The Time Machine.*

Once you're into the habit of coming up with book ideas, one of the best ways to decide which to play with and which to ignore is to focus on those ideas that seem to insistently nag you. Each time you try to ignore the idea, it comes back a little more formed and shaped and insistent than before until eventually you have no choice but to sit down and write your story.

With nonfiction book ideas, consider first: Who is my audience? Is it men? Is it women? Is it men *and* women? It's worth remembering that men and women have different interests in what they want to learn from books.

Is the topic a big enough idea that twenty to thirty thousand copies of this book could be sold? Will my idea appeal to a broad, though distinctive, audience? A good rule of thumb is to think: Am I affected by this topic? And if not, is someone I know—a friend or relative perhaps—affected by it? Will people be passionate about the subject? If they're only mildly interested, they more than likely won't buy the book in large enough numbers to make it worth publishing.

## THE GERM OF AN IDEA

Here are a few quick ways to come up with ideas for stories, whether fiction or nonfiction:

- Scour newspapers, magazines, and other sources of current events; what are the implications for the broadest number of people in these ideas?
- Invent lives for strangers you observe as you go about your daily business
- Think about something that happened to you or someone you know. What would have happened if things had gone differently? How many times have we said, "If only . . ."?
- Spontaneously write an opening "hook" or sentence
- Rewrite fairy tales and legends as modern stories.

As you can see, ideas are relatively easy to find once you start looking.

Now, let's say you have an idea. Some nonfiction ideas work well as articles in newspapers or magazines but don't hold up as books. So how can you tell what will make a book and what will make a successful article?

First of all, to make a successful book, even if it's a negative idea, say about those who are facing imminent death or about debunking popular myths, you need to find a positive spin on the topic. People don't want to spend twenty-odd dollars to be told things are dreary and impossible to achieve; they want to get some intimation of how to solve the problem.

A great example of how to do this is *The Physics of Star Trek*, by Lawrence M. Krauss. Instead of telling us that warp speed is impossible or that we will never develop the ability to beam people from one place to another, Krauss takes an idea and tells us what we would have to do and the laws of physics we would have to deal with in order to achieve so-and-so. The difference in going from a negative spin to a positive spin on the same idea is a fascinating and imaginative adventure into the realms of higher science as opposed to spending time with someone who constantly tells you what can't be done and that there's no future in thinking it can be done.

Once you have your idea, you are cultivating the germ, the first cell of an organism that eventually will take on a life of its own and become a book. That germ can end up being a major element in the story.

For example, every day on your way to work or shopping, you pass an abandoned Quonset hut, and eventually you write a story about a homeless family that moves into that hut. The germ of the story can also end up being a small part of the story, for example, a heist story that climaxes when the police chase the thieves into an abandoned Quonset hut.

The germ can also be something that never makes the cut into the final version of the story. For example, in the final draft of your heist story, you get rid of the Quonset hut and have your robbers run into McDonald's instead. It doesn't matter. The germ is just the thing that got you going.

As you develop your idea, there are certain things about this germ, this idea of yours, that you should question. Ask yourself, Is it a good idea or a bad idea?

## WHAT MAKES A BAD IDEA?

Let's look at the qualities of a bad idea first. Most bad ideas come into existence because the writer was drawn to them for the wrong reasons.

There are three things that can tip you off that your idea is probably a bad one. Apply what Gary called his F.I.T. test:

Familiarity
Importance
Truth

Let's start with *Familiarity*. Students would come up to Gary and say things such as, "I've got a fabulous idea for a book. My cousin has a niece who has a brother who's robbed six or seven Laundromats. I'll write a book about him, and with all the money I make, I'll be able to pay for his legal defense."

What's wrong with that? Well, unless you're related to Jeffrey Dahmer, O.J. Simpson, or someone equally notorious people are clamoring to read about, just because your cousin's nephew's aunt's brother did something "dodgy" that you know about doesn't mean it's a good idea for a book. Any good fiction writer could invent something like this.

This also applies to narrative nonfiction, which (unlike journalism where the event itself is the important piece of information to focus on) is about the *meaning* of the event. It's what you make of the event, how it affects you as a person, that's significant.

The second quality of a bad idea is *Importance*. An idea may be important to you because it comes from your life. But just because you have particular access to something doesn't automatically make it a good idea. A lot of times people will come up to me and say something such as, "I've spent twenty years in this company where they freeze-dry coffee. I'd like to write a book about this experience." Great. Apart from the fact that maybe you've got a permanent case of caffeine jitters, now what?

A less frivolous example is the woman who watches her husband slowly waste away from cancer, and when he's gone she has this "great idea" and decides she will write about a woman watching her husband die of cancer for two years.

This is a literary agent or editor's nightmare. You hate to tell somebody that a wrenching experience such as that or, more generally, the first twenty years of her life is not interesting enough to sustain even an article, let alone a good book idea. But the fact is, we've all been doing something for twenty years: making pizza, drilling holes in umbrella handles, whatever. Am I saying you can't write a good book about someone dying of cancer? Of course not. What I am saying is that because it is an important subject to you does not automatically make it a good idea. Such books are often a form of therapy (writers write, after all, at least partly to make sense of their lives), and the project will likely be doomed by the very sentiments that inspired you to write it.

Certainly, any idea you want to write about should be important to you, but it doesn't automatically follow that any idea that is important to you is a good idea. Don't throw yourself into an idea on the basis of that.

Which leads us to the third quality: *Truth*. Just because it's true doesn't make it a good idea. If editors and agents had a nickel for every time a beginning writer responded to criticism with a plaintive, "But it's *true*," we'd all be *very* wealthy people.

"But my cousin Jake really *was* married nineteen times," you say. Well, sometimes an idea that's true isn't even necessarily believable. In any case, you could make up a story about a guy who's been married nineteen times and it really wouldn't get you very far.

So remember, when you're working on developing story ideas, don't have a F.I.T.: Familiarity. Importance. Truth.

What these three things have in common is that they are based on the writer's needs. They make it easier for the writer; he doesn't have to do research; he doesn't have to "make stuff up." None of them are based on the reader's needs or wants.

Another test: Have you come across your idea in someone else's books or seen it on TV or in movies? If so, chances are it's not worth writing about because someone's beaten you to it. Occasionally, though, you can find ways to put a fresh spin on an existing idea.

## RESHAPING EXISTING IDEAS

Jim, a student of Gary's, had the idea that a wildlife biologist (who was part Sioux and a student Native American shaman) would help reintroduce the timber wolf into the wilds of the United States. As is the case in many werewolf novels, people start dying in nasty ways, and it is found that among the wolves, there is a werewolf, the last of her breed.

Now, even when done well, this is a fairly familiar idea, and Jim and I discussed various ways to spin the idea and make it fresh. What we came up with was this: Suppose, instead of the bodies of the victims being humans, the bodies were those of wolves. And that in order to protect and save the last of the wolves, a female, from the human predators, the shaman has to shape-shift into a wolf form. But having done so, he can't turn back. So in the end, while the hero gets the girl, in this case the girl turns out to be a female wolf and the hero had to become a wolf in order to fulfill his destiny.

Clearly there was a lot more to Jim's plot than I mention here, and a lot more to the way we discussed reshaping it. The point is that we decided to shift around the idea until we came up with a fresh angle on a potentially tired story and theme.

So study your genre or your topic and know it well enough to be familiar with what's been done and what hasn't. What's fresh and new and yet familiar enough it can still fit into the main body of books published in this area? This is called looking for a *hole*, that is, something that hasn't been done quite that way before.

Umberto Eco's *The Name of the Rose*, for example, is really a kind of Sherlock Holmes novel. *What if* Sherlock Holmes was a medieval monk and Dr. Watson was his student?

Find a hole, and you will usually find a good idea in there somewhere.

## IDENTIFYING GOOD IDEAS

So what exactly are the reader's needs? What are some qualities of a good idea that will encourage a reader to plunk down twenty-five dollars (or six dollars for a paperback) to buy your book?

Here's another of Gary's acronyms: W.A.G.S.

W.A.G.S. stands for **W**orld, **A**ctive, **G**oals and **S**takes.

### World

This is the narrative world to which you will take your reader. People read fiction and narrative nonfiction (such as biographies) to escape their lives. Strong stories, whether fiction or nonfiction, take you to new worlds and introduce you to new and interesting people and ideas. A guy who works at an insurance company all day long doesn't want to come home and read about an insurance company.

This guy wants to read about how characters resolve high-powered ethical and moral dilemmas he hopes he will never be faced with but that call up powerful emotional responses: Do I save the three hundred people on the approaching train that will crash if I don't lower the bridge, and crush my six-year-old daughter who has crawled out onto the track and gotten stuck? Or do I save her and kill all the people on the train instead? Welcome to my world.

Perhaps you've heard editors talk about "a sense of place." The world you create can be centered around an occupation, such as a high-powered law firm, or around a school, a ghetto, a jungle. Your world can be Gary, Indiana, or Flint, Michigan, but your story should be set there for a reason, not just because you happen to know the area well. What's unique about the place?

For example: What if an out-of-work auto mechanic found himself in a situation where he was forced to become an amateur private eye? The story would have to involve car manufacturing or other things connected to Detroit, or Flint.

The world of the movie *Tootsie* is a TV soap opera. The world of Michael Crichton's *Jurassic Park* is a theme park. Indeed, the world doesn't even have to be a physical location. The worlds of the TV shows *ER* and *Chicago Hope* are not just hospitals, but medicine. The world of Dick Francis's novels is horse racing, while Jackie Collins writes about the world of Hollywood glamour.

Most people want to go someplace exotic and foreign, somewhere with vivid colors and strong smells, and strange stark differences from the world they currently live in. They want to go to Istanbul, go to the set of a movie being made, follow a homicide cop on the job, go to an advertising firm, something of that sort. It's important to remember, though, that you don't have to have lived the life to write about it. You need to be willing to interview people who have lived in the world you propose to write about, and you need to research it thoroughly.

So, your story should be unique to your world. A good rule of thumb is that if you can move your story to another location, or world, you are not using the unique qualities of the story's setting to your advantage, and your story will have no personality or character that makes it stand out.

## Active

The second element of a good idea is active characters. You don't want to write about some woman who returns from Saudi Arabia and sits down for dinner and everyone tells her what's gone on while she's been away. She's then a passive character. You want her to be the character who takes action. Look at Bruce Willis in the movie *Die Hard* (from a novel by Roderick Thorp). What if he had called the police and stayed put, hiding from the bad guys and waiting for the police to arrive? Then we would have a story about the policeman who came to save everyone, not the John McClane character.

Movies and stories, both fiction and nonfiction, are told about the person who takes action, not the person who sits back and watches, observing the action without getting involved or just reacting to the events of the story. So make sure your characters are active and really do something to affect what's going on in the story. It's not what happens to the character that makes her interesting. It's what she does about it. Without an active character, there is no emotional power to your narrative. In a word, it becomes a boring story.

## Goals

We'll look at this subject in depth in chapter six. For now, think about whether your characters have clear and definable goals, goals that can be visually dramatized on the page. Ask yourself, What does this character want? It should be something specific and imaginable.

Here's an example: A character's goal is inner peace. That's what he's moving toward. He wants to be peaceful and calm.

By itself, this isn't a visually dramatic (or even active) goal. However, if the character is going to acquire this inner peace by climbing Mt. Everest, it's a different story. If he's going to fight the snow, the cold, the wind, exhaustion, and everything else, that's fine. If he's going to acquire this goal of inner peace by going to the jungles of Guatemala as a doctor for some impoverished people, that's fine, too. But if he's going to acquire inner peace by sitting in a temple and meditating for twenty years, that's not good. That's not a goal you can make visually dramatic.

## Stakes

The last quality of a good idea is stakes. High stakes. If you're asking people to sit down and read a three-hundred- or four-hundred-page book, devote many hours of their time, pay twenty or twenty-five dollars for this thing in hardcover, there had better be something really important at stake. If there's not, your readers aren't going to care enough to commit to your book—and what's worse, will be angry and disappointed if they don't think they have received a good enough payout for their investment of time and money and their expectations.

Take, for example, Ian Fleming's James Bond novels. World peace is always at stake. (James Bond stories are really a hybrid of World War II commando action stories and hard-boiled private eye stories, set in peace time. Fleming puts us on the front lines of the cold war at its hottest.) Thousands of people are going to die, the oceans are going to be poisoned forever, and readers get excited and compelled to read the book or watch the film.

If, in a James Bond story, the villain's main goal is to poison pigeons, do you think anyone will bother to read the whole story to find out whether the goal is reached? Of course not. The stakes aren't high enough. (It's worth mentioning, though, that a short story about an old man who is trying to protect local birds from some bird hater is potentially a good idea. It's all a matter of proportion. In a short story, where the reader's commitment is relatively short, you can get away with stakes that are relatively small, as long as they are high to the character. Life and death, everlasting love, the fate of nations—these are things the reader can care about.

In many ways, stories, whether true or invented, can be thought of as biographies of watershed events in the central character's life. The story begins when the trauma, or watershed event, begins, and the story ends when the trauma is resolved, or the watershed event ends. And because it's about a character, it also involves readers' emotions for and about this person.

As we go along we'll talk about conflict, resolution, and tension. Apply everything we talk about to your idea and ask yourself whether your idea is able to take in these concepts. Can it be made to fit the examples of successful dramatic structure we'll discuss? Having done that you'll know what to keep and what to leave out.

## EXERCISES

1. Write a word, then write another word, but don't try to associate it with the first word. Just write the first thing that pops into your head. Now try to put these words together into a single, somewhat coherent idea. Having done that, ask yourself, Does this idea have the qualities talked about here?

Does it have an interesting, new world or sense of place to which you are bringing the reader? Does it have active characters who really take control of their own fates and do whatever needs to be done? Does it have goals that can be made clear and definable; can the reader look at the page and say, "Yes! He just reached his goal!" because the reader (and the character) knows what it is? Does the idea have high stakes? Life-and-death matters? Love? Something, anything, really important at stake? Something that will make readers care about what happens to the characters and become emotionally involved in their lives?

2. Take a notebook and pen to a cafe or a mall. Sit in a corner and study people. Use "What if . . . ?" or "Suppose . . . ?" statements to generate ideas about what you imagine to be their stories.

*Chapter Two*

# Understanding Genres

I walked into a book superstore the other day, and it was wonderful to just wander around the maze of bookshelves, taking in the thousands of book covers and book titles lining the shelves. It was almost a churchlike feeling.

Being around all those books can somehow be comforting in a way I can't really explain. I've felt like this about books since I was seven or eight years old and used to go to the local library every week, either with one of my parents or, eventually, as I grew older, on my own. Many writers feel similarly—I know that Gary did, for example.

There are *so* many books in print (an average of fifty thousand a year are published in the United States alone by one count): Some are hardcover (sometimes called cloth); many more are paperback, both mass-market (the small-sized books that fit in your pocket) and trade (the larger-sized ones that almost look like hardcovers). All are different from each other but have one thing in common: Each book can be slotted into a category, or genre.

## BROWSING THE GENRES AND CATEGORIES

"Category" and "genre" are marketing terms that mean, more or less, the same thing. Their purpose is basically to help you find more easily what you respond to and like. They are also guidelines that let you know, generally, what you can expect to find in a certain type of book.

Genres developed as a way of marketing and selling mass-market paperbacks. As a result, even mainstream novels, when reprinted as mass-market paperbacks, need to be slotted into a genre of some sort.

Browsing bookshelves with an eye to studying genres can be very revealing, especially if you're thinking about writing your first book.

A common mistake an inexperienced writer can make is to assume that because, for example, romance develops in his cop novel, then the book must also be a romance. That's why, when you ask such a writer what his book is about, he often says, "It's about this thing, but also that thing, and maybe a third thing as well."

If you decide to write a crime novel, think about what it is that's always true about these stories; what it is that's always true about romance, always true about a comedy. In comedy, for instance, one of the conventions is nobody really gets hurt, although in black comedy, which is a variation of satire, this is not necessarily true.

When we talk about genre, we are referring to the main focus of the type of story that's being told. If your story is set on the American Frontier in the 1880s, and it involves ranchers and squatters, and gunfighters and greedy railroad barons, etc., you are writing a western. It doesn't matter if the hero falls in love and has a torrid affair with one of the robber baron's daughters; it's not a romance *unless the main focus of the story is squarely centered on the romance between the two characters.*

You could have a story about two cowboys who come across evidence that a werewolf is attacking and killing first their cattle and then settlers. This might be considered a cross-genre novel, but really it is just a horror novel set in the American West. Similarly, a story about a cowboy who has to solve the murder of a friend would be a mystery or crime novel with a western setting. Historical mysteries such as this are popular because they take readers to strange new worlds and the crimes involve elements from that world that while familiar in some ways are also refreshingly different and unpredictable in many others.

Let's browse some of the stacks in this bookstore.

## Romance

Romance fiction has a strict form, usually variations on girl meets boy, girl loses boy, girl finds boy again. You can write to the publishers of such fiction and they'll send you guidelines that will tell you how they like their books to be structured, how long they should be and so forth. Many romances are written by women, but certainly not all. In fact, Gary wrote a romance titled *Share the Dream* under the pseudonym Marian Chase.

All genre books feature cover illustrations that help sell the books. Romance novels often have muscled, bare-chested heroes à la Fabio cradling beautiful heroines who are falling into their arms. In general, the reader of romance fiction expects that both the hero and heroine will be alive and well and thoroughly in love with each other at the end of the story. They also shouldn't be separated for long periods of the book, and the story should end at a point in their story where there is the most hope for their relationship.

Why is the romance genre so popular? According to Kensington Senior Editor Kate Duffy, quoted in *Editors on Editing* (Grove Press), "If romance were as common as rudeness, I'd be unemployed." In other words, it touches something that we're all looking for in our separate ways. The quality of the book is determined by the perceptiveness of the writer and his ability to put words on paper. It's also true that you need to be able to create strong female characters who speak to the genre's readership, which is predominantly female.

There are different types of romances: Arabesque is a line of romances written specifically for an African-American audience. Regencies take place in the early 1800s. There are time travel adventure romances, such as Diana Gabaldon's *Voyager*, offbeat romances, such as Robert Waller's *The Bridges of Madison County*, and many more.

What they all have in common is the story of two people who fall in love. At the heart of every romance is how a relationship between a woman and a man develops into love and the problems that men and women have communicating with each other and negotiating their roles in a relationship.

If you read romances, it's a good field to break into as a writer, with a strong supportive network for novice writers from groups such as Romance Writers of America.

## Horror

The biggest-selling novelist of the last decade is probably Stephen King, followed closely by Anne Rice and Clive Barker. Horror fiction, once a part of science fiction and fantasy, has grown up to become a major genre in its own right.

Horror fiction has been best described by author Peter Straub as, "The thin ice of life." While it was a strong selling genre for authors to break into a couple of years ago, recently the only horror novels that are being published are from the well-established writers. What is horror's premise? To take everyday things and events and magnify them, exposing readers' fears so they can examine them safely. Ultimately, horror is about confronting and dealing with fear of death. Appropriately, the covers of horror novels often feature a combination of skulls and skeletons and fanged creatures dripping blood.

## Historicals

The serious historical novelist needs to be able to weave a fictional plot into real historical events without distorting the historical characters who appear.

To succeed, both fiction and nonfiction in this area has to be written by a recognized scholar, or someone with credentials of some sort, as for example a Ph.D. You can have other credentials, though. A parish priest could write a major work on religion and get it published; a teacher could write a book about education; a journalist could do a book about, say, the medical establishment; a parent of a sick child could have researched all there is to know abut the disease and then write about it. At the end of this book you'll find a sample nonfiction proposal about dyslexia that is exactly in this category. You need to have some edge, however small, beyond your interest in the topic, though. In general, those who are passionate about something also tend to have studied it a lot and are often experts by default.

The appeal of the historical novel is often the chance to meet real people as they really were. The historical writer also strives to maintain the customs, culture, and mind-set of the period. In a time of political correctness, it is sometimes difficult to maintain the integrity of portraying cruelty, ignorance, and hardship which clashes heavily with contemporary values. Perhaps for that reason historical novels are much tougher to write and sell now than previously.

The historical novel has relevance because of what the past has to tell us about the present. Arthur Miller's play *The Crucible*, about the Salem witch trials, was written in the early 1950s, but is also an allegory about the McCarthy House Un-American Activities' Committee witch-hunt for Communists. Most historical novels are best slanted to other genres, such as historical romance or historical mystery to make them more marketable.

## Crime Novels

Here's another aisle of books. *Baffled in Boston*, Gary's last murder mystery, appears in the mystery section, sometimes also known as the crime section. This is a popular genre with millions of devoted fans. There are "tough guy" mysteries, sometimes called "hard-boiled," such as those written by Raymond Chandler, Dashiell Hammett or Mickey Spillane, which feature a cynical private investigator or PI; or soft mysteries, sometimes called "cozys," usually featuring an amateur sleuth and typically along the lines of an Agatha Christie, John Dickson Carr or *Murder, She Wrote* kind of puzzle story.

Then there are police procedurals, where the usually gritty detail of what cops do to bring a criminal to justice is more prominent than the puzzle. One of the first examples of this was Ed McBain's 87th Precinct series. These days, most mystery editors agree that successful new mysteries are more concerned with interesting characters and setting than just an intriguing "puzzle."

## Thrillers

If the genre is thriller, we're going to have a protagonist who is in a lot of danger, what Stephen King called, in *Misery* (his horror novel about how to write fiction, believe it or not), "get out of that" storytelling. The car is about to go over the cliff, with our hero lying unconscious in the backseat. Get out of that . . . Every time the protagonist does something in a thriller, it is like going from the frying pan into the fire, danger on every single page; an organization or somebody is trying to get this protagonist. Readers of this genre of book expect this type of convention, and if you don't provide it, you're going to create a disappointing book. There are classic thrillers you should be familiar with, such as John Buchan's *The Thirty-Nine Steps*, Richard Condon's *The Manchurian Candidate* and Frederick Forsyth's *The Day of the Jackal*.

## Science Fiction and Fantasy

By the early 1990s, Science Fiction and Fantasy books were multibillion dollar generators of profit for publishing houses. Science Fiction (SF) and Fantasy, while around for a long time, took off as a genre after the striking success of the movie *Star Wars* in 1977. In many ways it has also paved the way for how publishing in general developed in the 1990s.

SF and Fantasy are "author driven," which means, simply, that readers pay attention to who wrote the book they last read and enjoyed and make efforts to find something else by that author. Author-driven material overcomes one of corporate publishing's biggest problems: how to mass market a commodity (that is, a book) in an industry that for most of its existence has been defined by its idiosyncratic nature. The generalized approach to selling books through the cult of the author as personality, which is now dominating publishing, first developed in the SF and Fantasy genre and spread to the others as its marketing success grew.

SF and Fantasy is a genre of contradictions: While *anything* is possible in an SF or Fantasy novel, and the phrase "cutting edge" is applied to almost every new writer of SF, there is, nevertheless, a powerful force of conservatism among SF and Fantasy editors. Many of the people involved in publishing SF and Fantasy cling to the notion that aping the success of others is more important (because of potential financial rewards) than encouraging the development of what HarperPrism Executive Editor and Vice President John Silbersack describes as the "literature of revolution." He explains, "The core purpose . . . of any work of fabulism . . . is the questioning of established things. SF takes this principle to extremes" (*Editors on Editing*, Grove Press). More than perhaps any other genre, there is a purity about SF fiction because SF and Fantasy are, in essence, fiction of ideas and experimentation.

One well-known SF series started with a book called *Dune*, by Frank Herbert, which was followed by *Dune Messiah*. Then there's *Children of Dune*, *God Emperor of Dune* and others. You'll notice that the covers of these books are quite different from the covers of romance novels. It's easy to see that *Dune* is a book about a desert planet and alien races and that it takes place in the future. You wouldn't confuse *Dune* with *Share the Dream*.

There are many kinds of Science Fiction, from the hard science type of story, to "space operas," such as *Star Wars* and *Star Trek*, to cyberpunk written by authors such as William Gibson and K.W. Jeter, to what can be called "head" science fiction or speculative fiction, where the science may be almost nonexistent.

Among the most famous Fantasy novels are The Lord of the Rings trilogy, by J.R.R. Tolkein; the Thomas Covenant series, by Stephen Donaldson; and the witty Belgariad series, by David Eddings. Then there are the science fiction/fantasy novels of C.J. Cherryh and Anne McCaffrey among many others.

## Westerns

Here's a famous book: *Shane*, by Jack Schaefer. Another is *Journey to Shiloh*, by Will Henry, and a third, *The Virginian*, by Owen Wister. By the covers, often showing cowboys with sidearms, Native Americans in full warpath regalia, wagon trains, and rearing horses against backgrounds reminiscent of the American Southwest, they, and the other books they are collected with, are clearly definable as westerns—that peculiar brand of story that is partly gritty, partly historical, partly mythological in its storymaking about the western frontier of America from roughly 1840 to 1900.

The West is a state of mind to most who live there and those who write about it (and several successful western authors have never been farther west than Newark, New Jersey!). The western is about the opening of the frontier, the perils and tribulations of creating something from nothing and those who gambled, often with their lives and their fortunes, in order to establish themselves and their dreams. There is a natural conflict at the heart of every western, be it man against man, man against nature, or man against himself. These conflicts are concerned with morality and the challenges of survival. The stories are filled with concepts such as sacrifice, self-denial, and unwavering commitment to a goal or an ideal, concepts that have a direction and clarity contemporary stories sometimes lack, for whatever reason.

Furthermore, they are, on one level (or should be), historical novels about people who existed in a specific time and place, and the novels should reflect just enough accurate historical detail to convince a reader he is in mid-nineteenth-century America.

Westerns are not an easy genre to break into, though, because there are only a handful of editors working in the field, and their lists are already pretty full.

## The Literary Novel

Literary (or mainstream) is a genre like any other. Some practitioners of this genre, though, believe that story is not important, and that writing and atmosphere are all. Literary novels are hard to sell because the competition and standards are extremely tough and the available publishing "slots" relatively few. The reason is that the publisher can't find an identifiable audience. There's no group that says, "Hey, do you have any mainstream novels?"

*The Shipping News*, by E. Annie Proulx; *A Portrait of the Artist as a Young Man*, by James Joyce; *For Whom the Bell Tolls*, by Ernest Hemingway; *The Name of the Rose*, by Umberto Eco; *Jazz*, by Toni Morrison; *The Joy Luck Club*, by Amy Tan; and *Slaves of New York*, by Tama Janowitz, are all good examples of literary novels. Some people confuse *literate* with *literary*, but they're not the same things. All books, whether fiction or nonfiction, should be literate, that is, gracefully well written.

The literary genre is a "tough nut to crack" for first-time writers. The literary novel must survive on the reputation and consummate skill of the writer, on book reviews and blurbs from other more famous writers, and on word of mouth. If you're a beginner, you don't have much of that going for you. There are plenty of examples to prove us wrong over the years, but then the authors are probably not reading this book, and almost certainly are not making a living writing fiction exclusively.

If you're writing a literary novel, consider whether it can be made into a novel of a more commercial genre. Maybe there's a romance in it. If so, build up the romance. Maybe there's a mystery—build it. After all, what made the great writers of the past "great" was not just their ability to paint images on the page with words and create memorable characters, it was their skill at spinning a good story. A lot more people have read Dickens or Twain or Tolstoy or even Joyce than Marcel Proust or Virginia Woolf because the former have a story to tell with wonderful, emotionally involving characters. James Joyce actually said that all stories should begin, "Once upon a time . . ."

## Nonfiction

Here's a nonfiction book: *How the Tiger Lost Its Stripes*, by Cory Meacham. It has a picture of a tiger on the front cover, and it's about the demise of the wild tiger. You can tell right away it's not going to be confused with Mario Puzo's *The Godfather* (which, while a mainstream novel, is really also a type of crime novel).

The cover blurbs or quotes and the title of the tiger book suggest that it might appeal to those who are interested in travel, the clash of cultures between East and West, the environment, and even books about cats. This is a popular science title, and it falls into a category that has its own rules and structure that must be observed and followed if you want to be published in it.

Narrative nonfiction, that is, character-driven nonfiction has a definite structure that needs to be considered. A good commercial nonfiction piece should have a narrative thrust, and it should encompass a debate on a topic of national interest that grows from the story. A good example of this would be *The Burning Bed* and the issue of domestic abuse. It should also find a positive spin on even the most negative topic. Readers don't want to plunk down twenty-five dollars for a book only to be told that life is hopeless. While that approach can work effectively in a magazine or newspaper because it is balanced by other more upbeat pieces in the same issue, a book rises or falls on its own merits.

A book of nonfiction must have lots of information and can't just be a soapbox for you to spout your pet grievance. If, for example, you're going to write about your struggles to get good medical care for your wife who is suffering from cancer, there's no point ranting and raving about the HMO that has made your (and your wife's) life miserable. You need to carefully recount, in as honest a way as possible, a strongly written narrative infused with lots of emotional content about what it was like to be unable to reach the HMO and complain about its inadequate care of your wife while she writhed in pain before you. People have to trust you as a guide to the topic you're writing about before they'll bother to read what you have to say. That's why most successful nonfiction is written by experts of one sort or another.

### True Crime

True crime is another nonfiction section in the bookstore. The experts who write true crime successfully are, or have been, lawyers, cops, investigators, journalists, forensic specialists and so forth. Let's take a look at the book *Witch Hunt*, by Kathryn Lyon. Looking on the back cover, I can see it is about a series of miscarriages of justice from overzealous police and prosecutors. William Styron, a famous writer I've heard of, is quoted on the cover as saying this is a terrific book. Several other writers whose work or reputation I know are similarly quoted. Perhaps I might buy this book. Cover blurbs or quotes on books, particularly books by new writers, can be very helpful in attracting readers to the book.

A few more well-known true crime narratives include *Charmer*, by Jack Olsen; *Small Sacrifices*, by Ann Rule; and the famous *In Cold Blood*, by Truman Capote. Is it nonfiction or fiction? It's a true story after all, though it was the first one to use fictional techniques to tell a true story.

True crime or current events books allow us to peer into the mind of the demented. They are influenced by whether a gripping story can be woven, who the characters are, where the story took place and so on. One of the elements of narrative nonfiction that many writers do not consider carefully enough is that it takes the techniques and skills of a journalist *and* a novelist to write a compelling story. *How* the story is told is as important as *what* happened.

In *Editors on Editing*, St. Martin's Press Senior Editor Charles Spicer explains there are two basic types of true crime book: the gut story, that is, one that affects us on a primal level, such as Ann Rule's *Small Sacrifices* about a mother murdering her children; and the glamour story, set in the world of the rich and famous, such as William Wright's *The Von*

*Bulow Affair* about the murder trial of Claus Von Bulow, accused of killing his socialite wife, Sunny.

Beyond powerful—and, of course, accurate—characterization with identifiable villains, and if possible also heroes, the narrative nonfiction book should have some sort of unraveling investigation. It is the writer's job to learn the art of the newspaper reporter, capturing not only the spirit of what was said and done, but doing it accurately without boring readers with unnecessary detail or speech.

## Fashion in Genres

True crime is an example of a category that, while once very popular, is now harder to sell. Fashion in genres goes in phases. A genre can be "hot," and then it is overbought and becomes hard to sell into for a while. The genre becomes "dormant" until a book comes along that reinvigorates the category beyond the work of the established few authors who have luckily continued to write and sell in that area, keeping it "ticking over." True crime books can sometimes be reshaped as current events if the story (such as *The Burning Bed*) is broad enough and symbolic enough to become more than just the sum of what happened.

## Biography

Biographies fall into many categories. For example, psychological biographies, such as Katherine Ramsland's biography of Anne Rice, *Prism of the Night*, use the work and life of the biographical subject as an indicator of the subject's inner world. Literary biographies such as A. Scott Berg's *Max Perkins: Editor of Genius* and Gerald Clarke's *Capote*, are always about literary figures.

There are broadly three types of biography. All try to reveal the essence of the subject: interpretive, where the facts of the story are interpreted by the biographer's imagination, in an effort to reveal the intimate qualities of the subject; objective, which gathers facts and documents how the subject lived;

and dramatic, which uses fictional techniques to re-create the subject and her times.

In general, a biography has to have a theme, and its subject has to fit into the context of the times the subject lived in. More than that, the subject of a biography should also be a symbol of some sort for the spirit of his age. The book should bring out some thematic element of that culture. Broadly, a good biography is one that illuminates and shows the times more than just the person.

The same kind of investigative, analytical attention to detail used in true crime is foremost in biography. The literary critic Roland Barthes once said that biography is fiction that dare not speak its name. The historian Doris Kearns Goodwin added, "The past is not simply the past, but a prism through which the subject filters his own changing self-image" (*Simpson's Contemporary Quotations*, p. 308:5).

The subject's life should have had a profound effect on the people who came into contact with her, and some shadow of it should also touch the reader of the biography.

The dangers of biography are inaccuracy and hero worship. The biographer needs to cultivate an objective eye that fits his subject into the world with compassion. Most biographies treat their subjects as one of three things: an example, a victim, or a source of wisdom.

It's not necessary, however, to tell a life in a chronological fashion. As with fiction, what is important is a series of illuminating scenes. In particular, readers need to see the formative scenes, in childhood or as an adult, that somehow throw a light on the subject's behavior and life. The death of Claudia, Anne Rice's child, was the catalyst through which readers can grasp Rice's life and events when they examine the world of her first few novels (*Interview With the Vampire*, *The Vampire Lestat*, etc.).

Biography depends on two things: public and personal papers and sources, and living witnesses. Of course, in the case of the long-dead, you're stuck with only one of the two. The biographer also needs to have the deepest regard for her subject, because undoubtedly the writer will discover that her subject has clay feet and is often disappointing on a personal level, especially when compared with the myth that may well have grown up around the subject. George Orwell's biographer learned, for example, that in person Orwell was a surly and unpleasant man.

It is perhaps one of the most demanding forms of writing: The author must know her subject intimately and must make certain that permissions are obtained from those relevant people who are living and that quotes are accurately related and sourced.

One of the best examples of a modern biography is *Anne Sexton: A Biography*, by Diane Middlebrook. Anne Sexton was a noted poet who had a history of psychiatric problems and who finally took her own life. The book received momentary notoriety when the first review in the trade magazine *Publishers Weekly* questioned the morality of using the tapes of Anne's sessions with her psychiatrist Dr. Martin Orne. Orne had agreed to cooperate with the author with the agreement of the Sexton estate, and he provided the private tapes for Middlebrook's use.

As Middlebrook wrote the biography (over ten years), she was able to relate Sexton's poetry to her psychiatric experiences, throwing new light on both Sexton and her work and helping us to appreciate both with greater understanding. Despite the controversy, the book received broad critical acclaim and became a best-seller.

The biographer must have the skills of a storyteller to construct an insightful, compelling narrative; a diplomat to deal with the many witnesses who can shed light on the subject's life; and a detective, in order to dig out facts and research on the subject. She must be devoted to her subject and yet objective enough to explore the dark nooks and crannies of the life in question. And she must have the literary brilliance and psychological insight to create a book that the subject could honestly admit was an accurate portrayal of who he is and what he is. Unless you are a skilled writer with a strong analytical background, biography is going to be a tough genre to use to break into publication.

## Memoirs

This is a particularly demanding form of autobiography, and deceptively difficult to write well. A big fuss was made of Kathryn Harrison's book about incest, *The Kiss*, and also Frank McCourt's memoir of a childhood cursed with drink, violence and poverty in *Angela's Ashes*.

In the wake of all this attention, a woman in my business partner Lori's building stopped her in the elevator one day and said, "I've written a memoir about growing up in this neighborhood. Would you like to read it?"

Now we get several manuscripts a week along these lines, nearly all of which we reject, so Lori asked her, "Was there any trauma in your family? Did you suffer rape or incest or serious disease?"

The woman was horrified and turned in a huff believing that Lori had slighted and ridiculed her. In fact, memoirs are about traumatic events in a writer's life that a writer of exquisite skill can transform into an experience we can all share. It is the nearest thing to poetry a writer of prose can create. Read Isabel Allende's moving book *Paula* about the sickness and coma her daughter suffered.

Memoirs are about a child's sickness, a father's death, a loss of honor or career. We read another's pain because the writer's sensibility allows him to extract from his dreadful experience powerful universal emotions that illuminate our lives. Editors who buy memoirs do so because the writers have successfully transferred their experiences to the page in a strong emotional way, and in so doing, like the alchemists of old, have transmuted the experiences from base lead into gold.

## NEARLY ALL BOOKS FIT A CATEGORY

Over by another stack of books, I've spotted one called *The Pork Chop War*, by Gary, aimed at children in the ten to thirteen age range. And here's another series of books aimed at young readers, *Goosebumps*, by R.L. Stine. Over there are some famous children's books: *Alice in Wonderland*, by Lewis Carroll, *The Lion, the Witch, and the Wardrobe*, by C.S. Lewis; and the Oz stories of L. Frank Baum.

Probably 98 percent of books written fall into some category. The reason for this is that readers gravitate toward a certain kind of reading encounter. You've probably had a similar experience. Perhaps there were periods when you read lots of westerns, then you started reading science fiction. Or you read a load of romances, and then Jackie Collins and some mysteries, and then you moved on to *Devil in a Blue Dress*, by Walter Mosley. Before you knew it, you were reading *The Kitchen God's Wife* by Amy Tan, and then novels by Alice Hoffman and Toni Morrison. But every time you went to the library or the bookstore, you had some idea of what you wanted to buy before you got there.

There are millions of people who love to read murder mysteries, for instance, and while they're looking for crime novels, they have no interest at all in reading romances or westerns. Perhaps the most recent books they read were murder mysteries and they enjoyed them so much that, while they don't want the same story, they do want stories with murders and crimes in them.

Similarly, if the last book you enjoyed was a romance, you'll likely go back to the store looking for that author's next book, or one like it. And so it's important for an author to understand what a reader's expectations are.

There are no formulas for writing category, or genre, fiction, because formulaic writing doesn't have the zing and pizzazz needed to get published these days. However, genre fiction does have individual conventions the writer must pay attention to in order to write a successful book. For example: In a mystery or crime novel, there must always be a crime or puzzle to solve.

"Genre thinking" is more and more a critical aspect of modern publishing. One of the first questions an editor asks of a manuscript is, "What is it?" What she means, of course, is, What genre is it? Once that's determined, the manuscript will be judged by the standards of that genre. So even if you've written an extremely intelligent western, for example, intelligence, while admirable, is not the point. What the editor is interested in is your ability to create convincing characters that speak to the readership. How well, and accurately, do you work in historical detail in an unobtrusive manner? How do you keep the reader tense and turning the page? To be successful you must study the books in the genre and define for yourself those qualities that helped to make the genre so special.

## WHAT'S YOUR GENRE?

Chances are your book idea falls into a category or that it's very close. If you understand what a reader's expectations are, you can make the book stronger and more likely to be sold to a publisher.

Of course, the reader's anticipation of something inside the book can be spoiled by something on the outside of the book, perhaps poorly chosen artwork (which you can't always control) or an inappropriate title. If you call your romance *Slasher From Hell*, you're not likely to attract readers who are looking for the type of experience you're providing, and the readers you do attract are going to be disappointed.

So, you want to be careful with titles, and you want to be careful with the language you use, making sure it's similar to other books in the category you've chosen to write in. (I'll talk a little more about this in chapter twelve.)

It's important you know your audience and study your category. Go to bookstores to familiarize yourself with the various genres, then read a lot of books in your genre of preference. In fact, if you're not reading the genre, you probably shouldn't be writing in it. Your first successfully published book will, almost inevitably, be centered around some category you really love. You don't "write what you know," as the old saw has it; you *draw upon* what you know. But you write what you read.

One of the things this category/genre business does is help the publishers and the bookstore owners know where to place your book in the bookstore.

When your novel comes out, you're not really competing with all the other books in the store; you're only competing with all the other books in your genre. So, without diverging too much from what's expected, you ought to be thinking about how you're going to make your book different from others in your category. And that difference comes from knowing your genre well enough that you can spot a "hole," or good idea, as was done with the idea of a historical murder mystery featuring Christopher Marlowe as a detective or with Walter Mosley's Easy Rawlins novels, such as *Devil in a Blue Dress*, about a black PI in the late 1940s.

## MEETING THE READER'S EXPECTATIONS

Know your audience. One of the biggest differences between books and other media forms is that movies and TV don't discriminate by age and gender. In general, books are written with a specific audience in mind. Self-help books, for example, have a strong female readership, while adventure travel books, such as man against nature (for example, *Into Thin Air* or *The Perfect Storm*) are bought and read mostly by men. Only those books that become big sellers transcend those limitations.

As I mentioned, each genre has its own conventions, that is, a set of expectations. Genres are not just confined to books. All forms of art employ categories. In classical music, for example, you can write an opera, a tone poem, a symphony, a concerto. Depending on the genre she chooses, a composer is also guided by the form of that genre, be it the sonata form, the fugue form, the AABA melodic structure common in popular music, or another form.

You can mix genres, coming up with what is called a cross genre. Ravel, Gershwin, Stravinsky, and Bartok borrowed heavily from other genres, such as folk music, spirituals, and gospel music, while jazz greats Duke Ellington and George Russell worked in the opposite direction, borrowing from classical forms. Each composer also influenced the work of others.

The same examples could be made in the visual arts. Graphic novels and comics are clearly influenced by, and influence, young filmmakers and many young writers. New forms often arise from the melding of two genres or the elevation of popular or familiar material. (Nobody has yet managed to blend three or more genres successfully, so the best advice is don't even try until you are experienced. Remember, keep it simple.) One of the great masters of mixing genres and raising popular trash to an art form was William Shakespeare. His command of poetry and insight into the human condition allowed him to blend bawdy comedy with fragile romance, combine powerful drama with Renaissance masques and turn medieval mystery plays (religious plays about good and evil) into something new and brilliant. Daniel Defoe in *Robinson Crusoe* and *Moll Flanders*, took the seventeenth-century equivalent of the kind of story that appears nowadays in the *National Enquirer*, and elevated it into art.

## DRAW ON YOUR EXPERIENCES

Part of what successful writing is all about is "seeing" the world around you. What I mean by this is appreciating your life experiences, not just for what happened, but for the universality of the experience that can somehow be incorporated into your story. The more readers can inject themselves into a story (often unconsciously), the more they connect to that story and that author, and the more vicariously enjoyable the reading experience becomes.

Even though plotting is important in writing, we are ultimately concerned with capturing characters—be they real people in true stories or fictional creations—so part of the art of "seeing" the world around us involves developing the ability to recognize character traits in ourselves and others and then going beyond clichés or stereotypes in order to capture on paper in a few short lines memorable portraits of people we encounter and experiences we endure. Those we meet and conjecture about become the models and sources of inspiration for the characters who people our fiction and allow us in our nonfiction writing to understand the unique elements of how we respond in stressful situations, such as the ones we are writing about.

A few years ago, Gary was famous, as he used to tell it, for the "fifteen minutes" that pop artist Andy Warhol said we will all experience. Gary became one of the finalists to replace newspaper advice columnist Ann Landers, and it was an exciting time with a lot of national television publicity attached to it. He didn't get the job, and the whole media circus eventually left town, but Gary decided to draw on that experience and write a novel called *Dear So-and-So*. It was, surprise, surprise, about a guy who gets involved in a contest to replace an advice columnist.

He wrote a few chapters and sent them around to various editors. The response was essentially, "Gary, we like your book, but it's mainstream and will probably sell about twelve copies. Do you think it could be turned into a category book? They are just so much easier to sell."

So, Gary went away, mulling over his disappointment, and decided he'd rather sell fifty thousand copies of a book than five, so he decided that, yes, indeed, he could make *Dear So-and-So* into a genre novel. So *Dear So-and-So* became *Dead So-and-So*. And in *Dead So-and-So* he managed to accomplish all the things he'd wanted to accomplish in *Dear So-and-So*. What he did was change the story to one about an advice columnist who dies. Her best friend, the narrator of the book, believes she was murdered, so he enters the contest to replace her in order to solve her murder. The happy end of this story is that mainstream *Dear So-and-So*, with some changes, became, eventually, *Baffled in Boston*, a mystery Gary was very happy to get published.

If you can take your mainstream book and turn it into a category book of some sort, I recommend it. Genre books are easier to sell, especially when you are not yet established on the literary scene. Of course, if you can't turn your book into a category of some sort, if you don't read category fiction of any sort, then you can't write it. You have to do what you have to do. If you're writing a mainstream novel and that's what you want to write, then go ahead and do it.

## EXERCISES

1. Read a book that falls into the category you're writing in—mystery, romance, thriller, whatever. As you go along, note all the things in the book that you think are in the other books of this type. These are the conventions of the category and should occur in your own book.

2. One of the best exercises in genre writing is to take a legend or fairy story and rethink it in several different genres. For example, the story of Perseus and his slaying of the Gorgon can be rewritten as a historical novel, a biography, a romance, a comedy, SF, etc. Make a list of categories, then take one story like this and write a synopsis for each category you came up with.

# Chapter Three

# Hooks

Ever thought of yourself as a fisherman, baiting, luring, and snagging your reader? Hooks bring to mind sharp metal objects with worms attached, wiggling invitingly to fish that become snagged fast on the end of fishing lines.

Hooking a reader is about catching that reader from the outset: no explanations, no setup or slow windup to your story, but bang—straight into it. It's about going for the jugular, in a literary sense; and some of the most susceptible readers to this form of writing are editors and agents. Hook them, and you'll get published not just once, but consistently.

## THE HOOK AS HIGH-CONCEPT IDEA

I represent the author William P. Wood who has established himself as one of the leading writers of legal thrillers. Two of his books have been turned into major movies, and several others are in development. As a former district attorney, he writes about areas of the law and lawyers that other authors of legal thrillers don't go into.

One of his books, called *Quicksand*, is about how federal cases are made and unmade. The story concerns a "power couple" whose feuding over their marital breakup spills into their public life. He is the head of a federal police task force, and she is his boss, a federal prosecutor. Both set their sights on an international arms dealer who plots a serious act of domestic terrorism. The arms dealer intends to achieve his goal by playing off the private feuding of the husband and wife in their professional life.

When I pitched the book to editors, I used the following marketing hook to get their attention: John Grisham meets Tom Clancy. Always ready for the next commercial best-seller, almost every editor's response without pause was, "Sounds interesting. Send it to me." Indeed, one bought it soon after.

Hooks are used all the time in Hollywood. There is a wonderful satire of this at the beginning of Robert Altman's movie *The Player*, which is about how a film producer quite literally gets away with murder in order to bring a story to the big screen. The opening crane shot of *The Player* is a satire of a shot devised by Orson Welles for the noir thriller *Touch of Evil*. In *The Player*, the camera swoops and soars like a snooping bug on a Hollywood lot, peeking through the windows of producers' offices while they're having story meetings. We eavesdrop on a variety of pitches writers are making to the producers for new movies. ("Think, a kind of Muppet version of *Die Hard!*" is typical of what one character says eagerly to a producer, oblivious to the idiocy of the idea.)

Hollywood types have a somewhat ironic name for this type of pitching: They call it the high-concept idea. The high-concept idea, you may recall, is a shorthand form of "story speak" used by writers, agents, publishers, and Hollywood types to encapsulate a story idea in as intriguing and simple a form as possible. Typically, it is a way of morphing two successful, familiar ideas to define the essence of a new, original piece.

Most stories are reminiscent of others. Indeed, a writer friend only half joking once said to me all stories can be reduced to two types: A stranger knocks on the door; and someone goes on a journey. So pitching high-concept ideas relies on a common reference language of successful movies or books (or ideas in general) that conveys a great deal more than just the titles used.

This is a form of cultural literacy. For example, when we talk about the scientist Sir Isaac Newton, we often make the assumption that the person we're talking with understands that by mentioning Newton we are also making a sort of short-hand reference to a story about Sir Isaac sitting under an apple tree, getting hit on the head by a falling apple, and discovering the principle of gravity. And that led to his affirmation that the sun, not the Earth, was the center of the solar system, the elliptical orbits of planets and so forth. Thus, by connection "Newton" and "Newtonian" have become terms we use in casual conversation that imply and encompass "gravity" and Newton's other scientific discoveries.

The high-concept hook is about pitching the marketability and originality of your idea. Walk into any large bookstore, and take a moment to appreciate the thousands of books on the shelves that radiate out from the front door where you're standing. With all those books already on the shelves, how are you going to single out *your* book, and get reader attention for *your* work? The answer is to start with a snappy, intriguing description that also manages to suggest information about the uniqueness of your story.

When you go to the video store to rent a movie, you don't usually get a chance to see what you're renting. Instead, what you tend to rely upon is the brief description of the film on the back of the box, and you make your decision, more often than not, on that description, not on the film itself. The same is true of books. If the flap copy, or sales pitch, for your book is flat because your conceptualization of your book's strengths is thin, your book won't get the best shot at reaching the widest possible audience.

By using a reference language of well-known ideas, you are relying, at least in part, on tweaking your readers' imaginations enough that they want to read the book (or film script, etc.), to see if their image of what this morphing of ideas suggests is actually what you managed to produce. Hopefully, what you wrote will be even better than they imagined.

They've taken the bait. Potential readers are taking the time to examine your work. They'll examine the blurb about the book, read the opening paragraph in the store, maybe flip through and check out some odd pages. They like what they

see. At each stage you have to hook readers ever more firmly
until, intrigued enough, they go to the cash register and plop
down hard-earned cash to fully experience whatever it is
you've written that will fulfill its promise. Do that successfully,
and readers will remember your name affectionately, and you
have hopefully started a trend of author recognition that will
spill over to your other books.

The hook is primarily about concept. If a writer fails to
fully conceptualize his book, he is asking to have it published
poorly, should it be bought at all. At one time, publishing
worked on the principle that an accepted manuscript would
be edited first by the acquiring editor then by a copyeditor.
Once in the system it would be assigned a publishing season
(such as spring or fall) and decisions would be made about
the jacket, marketing, advertising, publicity, print run and so
forth.

What is happening more and more, however, is that, because of the rushed nature of modern publishing, decisions
about *how* a book will be published are made before the finished manuscript has even been submitted to the editor. By
the time the copyeditor sees the manuscript, the only thing
the art department and marketing and sales departments are
interested in is the concept of the book, usually expressed in
the original proposal, or accompanying story synopsis in the
case of fiction. If that concept is thin or vague, the publishing
house won't be able to publish the book well because no one
will have the information needed to know why the book is
being written, what it's trying to do, and therefore why anyone
would want to buy it.

Conceptualization is the single most important thing a
writer can do to help a publisher publish a book well. In nonfiction in particular, it really isn't surprising that many of the
best titled books are also those that sum up the book's concept. Some examples of published titles that illustrate this are
*Consciousness Explained*, *The Overworked American* and
*The Rise and Fall of the Great Powers*.

## THE QUERY LETTER

When you sit down and write a query letter to an editor or agent, the hook you've come up with for your story is very important.

Writers often complain about having to compose query letters, and I hear all the time about how unfair it is that editors and agents seem to judge a manuscript not on its merits, but on the query letter, and worse, the one line or one paragraph hook that accompanies it.

What the hook does, apart from intrigue me, or an editor, is show me that your story has a specific focus and that the focus is original in thought—and most importantly, won't disappoint me when I read the manuscript.

Save me from yet *another* letter that begins, "Dear Mr. Rubie: What if a vampire got AIDS!" or, "Drug-dealing gangsters are killed by a vigilante librarian avenging her daughter's death from an accidental overdose." Good stories? Perhaps in the execution. But the fact is they are old and obvious ideas agents and editors see all the time.

If you can't write a compelling one-page query letter, how can you expect to write a compelling novel? It is not so much what a query letter says that catches an agent or editor's eye, it's *the way* it's said. In other words, its dramatic structure. The letter is, in effect, an advertisement for the degree of accomplishment of a writer's story sense and ability to write. A query letter also tells the publisher that you know precisely what a book is, what a writer does and so forth. In other words, that you are a professional. Many books fail to catch an editor's eye simply because the writer displays amateurism and creates in the editor's mind the fear that the author has no idea how to write a book, let alone how to write a good one.

## THE SAGA OF THE GOOD HOOK

A good one-sentence hook in a query letter describing a novel will catch the agent's eye, who, after reading the manuscript, decides to take on the book. In his submission letter to the editor, the agent will use that one-line hook because it influenced his decision to represent the book and the writer. The editor will read the book with enthusiastic anticipation because of that one-line hook. She will go to an editorial board and use it to convince her colleagues in editorial, sales, and marketing that this is a book they should buy not only because it is good, but, more importantly from the company's perspective, because it will make the company money.

When your book comes out, the publisher's sales representative will go to a bookstore and try to sell your book, along with ten or twenty others, to the bookstore buyer or, in the case of independent bookstores, the owner. He's going to have probably about a minute at most to describe your book and get the bookstore owner to buy copies. So what's the sales rep going to say in one sentence that's going to excite the bookstore owner to stock your book? What's the bookstore owner going to say to the customer to excite her about your book? You got it; more than likely, they'll use the hook you came up with in your query letter that got you an agent in the first place.

Before we get to examples of hooks, here are two query letter samples that exhibit the varying degrees of development of a writer's story sense:

Dear Sir,

I recently wrote a novel about a couple of twelve-year-old kids who end up killing a woman by accident when they sabotage the off-ramp to a turnpike. One of the kid's father, a mean fellow, ends up going to jail for murder after his son's friend frames him.

But now, twenty-one years later, Dad is getting out of jail and wants revenge.

This is a good idea, and I would probably ask to see a sample of the manuscript with a synopsis of the story. But the writing is not overly compelling and the presentation's frankly humdrum.

Now, the following is what the writer, Michael Aronovitz, actually wrote to me. The difference, as you'll see, is like night and day. From these few paragraphs on a one-page letter, I knew this was a writer with a potentially good book, and I eagerly looked forward to reading the full manuscript. See if you feel the same way:

Dear Mr. Rubie,

We never meant to kill her.

It was just mischief after all—two twelve-year-old boys passing time on an abandoned construction site and pushing out chests to see who would go farther. Kyle Jr. was the one with the bad reputation. It was his idea to flatten some passerby's tires and *he* brought along the box of bent nails . . .

It wasn't *my* idea to create that ambush at the bottom of the off-ramp, but before there was a chance for pro-test, a car came barreling down the unmarked exit, tires blown, a wounded bullet rocketing straight for a thick oak tree!

That memory has haunted me for twenty-one years, and it all exploded today in spatters of blood, black blood, the block print of a newspaper headline.

KYLE SKINNER SR. RELEASED.

The waiting will not be long now. . . .

At the end of the letter, he included a brief paragraph mentioning his short story publishing credits, which also made me feel this was a writer who was doing all the right things in his quest to get published and was someone whose work I wanted to read.

Which version excites and interests you the most?

Here are some examples of hooks. If you think they bear a strong resemblance to Hollywood's high-concept idea I mentioned earlier, you're quite right. But what a hook does is provide you with a clear beginning and strong focus for your work, as in these examples:

- What would you do if you could live your life over again, knowing what the future will be (the hook for *Replay*, Ken Grimwood)?
- When an advice columnist is murdered, her best friend wins a contest to replace her in order to solve her murder (*Baffled in Boston*, Gary Provost's last novel).
- A Memphis law firm is laundering money for the Mafia, and a young lawyer who tries to leave the firm is threatened with death (*The Firm*, John Grisham).
- Terrorists threaten to blow up the Super Bowl from a blimp (*Black Sunday*, Thomas Harris).
- A group of explorers, investigating disturbances at sea, are captured by the megalomaniacal captain of a high-tech deep-sea submarine (*20,000 Leagues Under the Sea*, Jules Verne).

The last example would not be very high concept now, but in its day—1870—it certainly was.

There's nothing new about high concept: A senile old man gives away everything he owns to flattering daughters who promise to look after him and then turn him out penniless into the streets once they have his money (*King Lear*, William Shakespeare). Or this one: On Christmas Eve, a miserly old man is visited by three ghosts who show him his past, present, and miserable future unless he mends his ways (*A Christmas Carol*, Charles Dickens).

Not every story has to be high concept, and not every hugely successful story has to be high concept, but the idea of marketing your work this way is becoming more and more important. A good example of a non-high-concept idea would be *The Catcher in the Rye*, by J.D. Salinger.

The book is, superficially, the story of a young man's expulsion from yet another school. In fact, it is really a perceptive study of one individual's growing awareness and understanding of who he is. Holden Caulfield, a teenager growing up in 1950s New York, has been expelled from school for poor achievement once again. In an attempt to deal with this, he plays hooky from school for a few days prior to the end of term and goes to New York City before returning to face what he knows will be his parents' anger. Written as a first-person monologue and influenced in style by James Joyce and Virginia Woolf, the book describes Holden's thoughts and activities over these few days, during which he undergoes a nervous breakdown, characterized by bouts of depression, and erratic behavior.

As you can see, it is a tough story to nail down in a sentence because it is so dependent on voice and literary merit. Its appeal is more to the intellect than the emotions, a much tougher kind of book to write and sell.

The importance of high concept to you is that it suggests a general attitude you should have about your work, particularly your fiction: the belief that things should be "big," that this journey will be an emotional roller coaster.

A story isn't real life, and very few writers manage to convincingly give us real life that is also dramatically and emotionally satisfying. Private detectives don't really solve murders most of the time. Secretaries from Des Moines don't really fall in love with millionaire horse breeders on vacation in Barbados.

Characters in stories are bigger than real people; they do what we wish we could do. You need to go for the jugular, on an emotional level. Characters should find the courage to act where we would be inhibited; they can have snappy comebacks to put-downs *when they occur*, not a day later sitting in the car at traffic lights. They are more articulate, their emotions are deeper, their actions are more theatrical. There is more at stake, greater urgency, deeper significance, than in most real-life situations. As you begin to develop your book idea, ask yourself, Is this something bigger than real life that I can make believable? You'll start to develop your hook from this.

## HOLDING THE READER'S ATTENTION

How about this for the opening paragraph of a book:

> Yossarian was in love. The first time he saw the Chaplain it was love at first sight.

Did that hook you? It certainly worked with millions of other people and turned the book into a best-seller that is considered a minor classic twenty-odd years after its first publication. It's the opening paragraph of Joseph Heller's best-selling antiwar satire, *Catch-22*.

What about this:

> It began on a night when he thought he was finished, when all he wanted was peace.
> "Here comes another one," the eager rookie sitting next to him said. "That makes five."

That's the opening sentence to John Westermann's cop thriller *The Honor Farm* (Pocket Books), about a special prison for dirty cops.

Grabbing a reader with a snappy description is only part of hooking a reader's attention. There are also techniques that can help to keep this interest level high. We will discuss a number of them in more detail as we progress through the book.

Think of the reader as that large fish you are carefully reeling in to the boat. You need to know when to keep the line taut and when to allow a little slack.

The best way to keep the reader hooked is by keeping the hero or protagonist of your story in constant conflict with his environment. This entails putting your main character through a series of changes in circumstance.

There must also be a lot at stake. What sells these days is fiction and narrative nonfiction of extremes.

This doesn't mean that things always need to be extreme in terms of events, but they should always be extreme in terms of the main character's emotional experiences. Your protagonist, in other words, must always care deeply about what is happening, what has happened, and what is likely to happen.

Here are some other suggestions for keeping the reader hooked:

• Each word, each sentence, each chapter should be aimed at your target audience. The "voice" of the story should not only be appropriate for the story you're telling, but should also be in harmony with the readers' expectations. Consistency is the key. If you write chapters in conflicting styles, you will no longer have the readers hooked; they will get bored and slip the line.

• One classic technique for keeping the reader hooked is to have some sort of "ticking clock"—a problem that has to be solved within a set period of time. The movie *D.O.A.* (Dead on Arrival) is a classic of this sort of story.

• Each chapter should end with some sort of *Perils of Pauline* cliff-hanging suspense. James Clavell's excellent novel *Shogun* is written with this kind of technique, each chapter dynamically leading into the next.

• In some novels, an element of the incredible can be made believable in order to keep the reader hooked and the line taut. In James Hilton's *Lost Horizon*, for example, an adventurer in the Himalayas stumbles into a fantasy world called Shangri-La, where people remain young for hundreds of years.

• Sometimes controversial material, when handled appropriately, can keep a reader hooked. For example, *The Adventures of Huckleberry Finn* attacks slavery, *Lives of the*

*Monster Dogs* deals with our need for conformity in society, regardless of the bizarre extremes we have to go to homogenize our world.

• Genre novels, rather than midlist fiction ideas, and an all-encompassing universal quality to a narrative nonfiction piece can create a sustaining interest that will carry readers through.

• How you tell your story is important. In one sense, all forms of narrative writing are detective stories: the sense of pacing of information, that is, what readers know about the details of the story and when they learn them. How you "peel the onion" will determine whether your readers remain hooked.

• Characterizations should be structured and interesting. Avoid the obvious and clichés.

• Of the four forms of narrative writing—exposition, description, narration, and cinematic action—it is action (that is, making sure things happen) that is the most important in keeping the reader hooked. Is something new happening on almost every page of your opening chapter? Make sure your main characters *act* rather than *react*, thus continuing to involve the reader at an emotionally visceral level that will keep her hooked on the end of your taut story line.

## EXERCISES

1. Think about your favorite books, films, myths, fairy tales, and so on, and practice writing one-line or one-paragraph hooks for them. The hooks should all begin, "What if," or, "Suppose." How many strong hooks for each story can you come up with?

2. What's the hook for *your* book? Think about the one-sentence synopsis—something exciting, something compelling—that will make me want to read the book. Write it.

3. Write a draft of the second chapter of your book. Consider throwing away your current chapter one and making this new draft chapter one instead.

*Chapter Four*

# **Plotting**

S
o, you want to tell a story. Where do you begin? You've got this idea, but you don't know what to do with it. You've refined your idea to a hook and you have a character, perhaps a couple, so at least you have a fairly definite concept of what you want to write about. If you don't, then go back and figure it out, at least broadly. If all you've got is, "I'm writing a family saga about three generations of Russians in Chicago," or, perhaps more subtly, "I'm writing about a group of kids who are suddenly banned from dancing every weekend," you still haven't got any real idea what it is you want to write.

Define your story idea with "What if . . ." or "Suppose . . ." and suddenly you have the missing ingredients—a character and a potential plan of action. The next thing to do is ask questions of your plot and characters. Why are they doing this now? Why is he here and not there? Why has she done this and not that? Examine the motivation of all the characters in your story, regardless of whether they actually appear on stage, and the viewpoint you finally choose to tell your story. (We'll talk more about viewpoint later.)

## THE STRUCTURE OF A STORY

Let's look at the structure of a story and see how that will help you build it.

Those of us who knew Gary Provost, including the many who studied with him, will recognize with a smile what we teasingly called the Gary Provost Sentence. In fact, I added some punctuation to make it a little easier to read, so below is the new and improved Gary Provost Paragraph:

> Once upon a time, *something happened* to some-one, and he decided that he would pursue a *goal*. So he devised a *plan of action*, and even though there were *forces trying to stop him*, he moved forward because there was *a lot at stake*. And just as things seemed as *bad as they could get*, he learned an *important lesson*, and when *offered the prize* he had sought so strenu-ously, he had to *decide whether or not to take it*, and in making that decision he *satisfied a need* that had been created by *something in his past*.

Sound familiar? It should. What Gary came up with is the plot for 90 percent of the stories you've ever read, 90 percent of the films you've ever seen—in fact, 90 percent of all stories ever told in all the world in all time. It's as true for narrative nonfiction as it is for fiction.

This is classic dramatic structure. It works because it's story-telling that is most satisfying to the reader. And in case you think this is a newfangled idea, it was actually first defined by an ancient Greek playwright named Aristotle. He maintained that good drama was storytelling that defined character, cre-ated atmosphere, and advanced the action of the plot. No one has ever really substantively improved on this beautifully sim-ple yet profound definition. For my money, Norman Mailer came close, when he said in an interview (*The South Bank Show*, Bravo Network), "The best fiction is where art, philoso-phy, and adventure all meet."

All narratives, whether fiction or nonfiction, need structure. Without structure a story wanders around in search of itself. And what's worse, it commits the ultimate crime a story can commit—it becomes long-winded and boring. A story must *start* somewhere and *end* somewhere, and in between it must move forward in a spiral-like fashion, with a clear-cut, forward-moving line of dramatic motion.

Let's go through Gary's paragraph again. This time I'll stop along the way and talk about the elements of plotting he discussed. Once you understand these elements, whether you're a literary novelist, a nonfiction writer, or a genre writer, you'll be much better prepared to plot a story.

## Once Upon a Time, Something Happened to Someone . . .

This is what we call the inciting incident. In other words, it's what caused the story to kick in. Say your story begins on Thursday. Don't begin it on Wednesday, just to "set the scene and introduce the characters," a classic amateur flaw. Plunge right into the action the moment it starts. Why? Because nothing significant happened on Wednesday. You're not writing someone's life; you're writing the story of a watershed moment in that life. The thing that happened to upset the equilibrium or the balance in his life is the thing that begins the story. That's the inciting incident. That's where your story should start.

## . . . And He Decided That He Would Pursue a Goal.

There's something this person wants. What is it? It's the prize, the thing he's trying to get to, all through the story. What is it your main character wants? In the long run, what does he hope to achieve?

## So He Devised a Plan of Action, . . .

Let's call this the strategy. How is your hero going to go about pursuing his goal, or prize? What's he going to do? What's his plan?

## . . . And Even Though There Were Forces Trying to Stop Him, . . .

This is the opposition, the conflict. Conflict is the basis of all drama. Your hero wants something, and he's figured out a way to get it. Something has to get in his way, something or somebody has to have a conflicting goal and a conflicting plan—something has to try to stop him. Nobody's interested in reading a story about a guy who wanted a million dollars and got it. People want to read about a guy who wanted a million dollars and had a lot of trouble getting it. There are forces coming against your hero; there is conflict. It is the emotional "temperature gauge" of your narrative.

### . . . He Moved Forward Because There Was a Lot at Stake.

Ah, the stakes: We've been introduced to what your hero wants, what plan he's devised to get it, and now we learn what this effort will cost him. Nothing of any importance in this life is free. In one form or another, we always pay a price for what we most desire. The stakes in a story have to be high. What are they in yours? Life or death, lovers lost forever, friends becoming implacable enemies—something important we can all relate to. You don't want to write a story about a guy who is going to lose his laptop computer or his comb. It's got to be something important, something big enough to disrupt his life, to change him from what he was into someone else by the end of the story. It's the emotional engine of your narrative. Characters become obsessive about their goals. What price will they pay to reach them?

### And Just as Things Seemed as Bad as They Could Get, . . .

This is known as the bleakest moment. Things are dark and dreary for this person. Everything has gone wrong, and it seems as if the forces of opposition arrayed against him have won. But somehow, from the darkness of his despair and depression, from his failures, he finds the strength to persevere and overcome against overwhelming odds. Again, you're ratcheting up the emotional power of your story.

### . . . He Learned an Important Lesson,

Aha, a revelation. Your protagonist comes through his bleakest moment with a gift—understanding. At last he *sees*, he understands something about life that he didn't understand before.

Stories are about people growing and changing, about their insights into the human condition. By the end of the story, this new knowledge has changed your protagonist for the better. He is a little wiser and a little stronger. He has a little more faith in himself or in others or in the bountiful nature of life. He has grown and learned a lesson. The narrative's success can be measured by how much readers care, how much they have become emotionally involved in this journey.

### . . . And When Offered the Prize He Had Sought So Strenuously, He Had to Decide Whether or Not to Take It, . . .

Again, you are dealing with an emotional quality in your storytelling. Your hero makes a decision. The important thing to remember about this decision is that when he makes it, he gains something and he gives something up. It isn't much of a decision if someone says, "Hey, here's a million dollars. You can take it or leave it." But if someone comes along and says, "Congratulations, now you can get your million dollars. But there's one catch: If you take it, you'll never see your daughter again. And if you want to keep on seeing your daughter, you'll never get another chance to get the million dollars you've just earned." Now this is an important decision your hero must make. It involves high emotional intensity from the reader, as well as moral and ethical considerations—the most compelling of story elements.

### . . . And in Making That Decision He Satisfied a Need . . .

Let's call this the hole. It is the emotional "engine" that has been driving the hero to do stuff the whole of his life, and certainly for the duration of the story, though he may not even be aware of what that hole is.

### . . . That Had Been Created by Something in His Past.

This is the importance of the backstory. The backstory simply means his past, whatever happened in his past relevant to the story you're telling. The need, or hole, is some event that involved your hero before the story began. Or perhaps it's some item that haunts him, as in *Citizen Kane*, with the enigmatic reference to the boyhood sled Rosebud. In some way the hero is still incomplete. He's been injured, or he's had a part of him taken away. Perhaps he's lost his faith or rejected love. Perhaps he's a loner, someone who's not good at sharing himself with others, and he comes into this story carrying this thing with him, needing this hole filled. And in the process of the story, the hole is filled as he comes to his realization.

## THE MODEL FOR YOUR STORY

Obviously what I've just discussed is a generic structure for storytelling and is really more of a guideline to help you determine a forward movement. It is a paradigm, or model, of dramatic structure. Certainly, your story should differ in various ways; we're not trying to encourage writers to write formulaic fiction. Remember, what we're talking about is structure, in the same way that there are specific requirements for building a house so that it stands firmly in all weather and is not in danger of falling down. As long as the building's structure (or in your case, the story's structure) holds firm, all is well. If it doesn't stand firm—and you have to rely on your instincts for this—you need to go back to the model and analyze why your story isn't working properly, using the model as a guideline.

Let's look at a couple of examples and see how this paradigm applies. We'll use a mixture of films and books, because many people are more familiar with movie versions of stories than books and because film structure is easier to analyze.

Consider *The Firm*, by John Grisham. At its heart, this is a retelling of the classic Faust story. Its emotional power derives from the struggle the hero undergoes with the substantial moral and ethical dilemmas he has to solve. The hero is a man who sells his soul to the Devil for the "good life," which is the thing he thinks he wants most, and then realizes what a terrible price he has paid for it and tries to get his soul back.

## Inciting Incident

The hero, an ambitious, poor kid from across the tracks and just out of law school, gets his dream job with a prestigious Memphis law firm. Then he realizes he's made a terrible mistake. The firm is a front for a Mafia family.

## Goal

The young lawyer must determine how to leave his job without getting himself or his wife killed in the process, and remain a lawyer and an individual with his honor and integrity intact.

## Strategy

He sees a way out of his dilemma: a cunning path that will allow him to maintain his ethics—lawyer/client confidentiality—and continue his life as he wants to, that is be a lawyer without being disbarred, retain his life without having to go into a federal witness protection program and look over his shoulder for a Mafia hit man the rest of his life, and nail the bad guys in the firm. He does this by collecting evidence of fraud, overcharged bills sent through the mail—a federal offence. This allows him to separate his law firm bosses from their Mafia clients, handing the lawyers over to the FBI who can charge them with federal crimes, while keeping intact his lawyer/client relationship with the Mafia bosses. Thus he retains his ability to continue practicing as a lawyer without the fear that the Mob will send someone to kill him one day.

## Opposition

The firm, particularly its security chief, has killed others who tried to leave and will kill or blackmail the hero to force him to stay.

## Stakes

The attorney must keep his life in a literal sense and get it back in a metaphorical one.

## Bleakest Moment

His wife leaves him and he sees no way out of a double bind: The Mafia has all but stolen his soul and enslaved him in a guilded cage, while the FBI wants him to trash his ethics and future as a brilliant young lawyer and will perhaps even send him to jail along with the other lawyers targeted in the firm if he refuses to cooperate.

## Revelation

Money, power, and all the trappings of the Yuppie materialistic world he thought he always wanted are nothing compared to the love of his wife, his ability to do what he loves best, that is, practice law in a meaningful way to help people, and maintain his honor and his ethics.

## Decision

The hero decides to give up all the material success he's achieved in favor of a simple, more honest and fulfilling life.

## Emotional or Psychological Hole

As a kid he was poor and seemingly powerless, growing up in a trailer park with an older brother in jail for manslaughter.

## Filling the Hole

He learns what is important in life and what is glittering illusion, becoming a more mature and complete person in the process.

Here are some other movies and examples of plotting elements:

• **Witness:** A young Amish boy witnesses a brutal murder, and a police officer (Harrison Ford) has to travel to Amish Pennsylvania to protect the child from the bad guys who have tracked him down.

The inciting incident is the murder in the train station the boy witnesses. Without the murder, there is no story.

- **48 Hrs:** A cop and a convict have forty-eight hours to find and arrest a psychotic thief who has murdered his way off a chain gang and gone north looking for the stolen money he hid.

The prize here, as in many cops and robbers movies, is the capture of the villain.

- **Tootsie:** A talented but unemployed actor pretends to be a woman in order to land a plum role on a daytime soap opera. The only drawback: He (Dustin Hoffman) has to keep secret the fact that he's a man as long as he is starring in the soap.

The Dustin Hoffman character can't get a job as an actor. So his strategy is to disguise himself as a woman and achieve his goal that way.

- **Close Encounters of the Third Kind:** A man is obsessed with a mountain he has never seen, and in his search to find it discovers he is one of several who have been chosen by extraterrestrials to represent the human race.

Everyone in the movie thinks this man (Richard Dreyfuss) is crazy and tries to prevent him from getting to the mountain to witness the arrival of the alien spaceship. Later the conflict gets even greater, because he reaches his goal of finding the mountain, only to discover the U.S. government and the military are conspiring to prevent him from taking the last step to reaching that goal. His prize? He is chosen by the aliens to go up in their spaceship.

- **The Great Escape:** Several hundred Allied prisoners of war in Germany in 1944 plot to escape their captors. The stakes are freedom or death and torture if they're recaptured by the Nazis.

- **The Fugitive:** Interestingly, the bleakest moment happens even before the opening credits of the film are finished. Richard Kimble (Harrison Ford) has been wrongly condemned to death for the murder of his wife. The scene of his bleakest moment shows him sitting on a bus on the way to prison, shivering with fear, his life as he has known it, gone forever through no fault of his own.

- **The Wizard of Oz:** A little girl and her dog are swept up from Depression-era Kansas by a tornado and deposited in a fantasy land called Oz, where she has to secure the legendary wizard's help to get home again.

All stories have lessons, and the most famous is probably from this film. It's true, it's obvious, and verging on moronic, but at the end of the film, Dorothy says something to the effect of: "I learned that when I go looking for my heart's desire, I don't have to go farther than my own backyard, because if it isn't there, I never lost it in the first place."

Now, to be honest, Gary and I used to discuss this particular example all the time, and neither of us could figure out exactly what it meant. Nevertheless, it's a clear example of a character coming out and announcing the lesson of the story in the most bald-faced way.

• **Lethal Weapon:** Undercover cop Martin Riggs (Mel Gibson), a borderline psychopath, is teamed with family-man cop Roger Murtaugh (Danny Glover) in order to nail a drug ring. In the process, Riggs has to rescue Murtaugh's teenage daughter from the clutches of the bad guys.

Mel Gibson begins the story as a tragic, driven character, whose actions verge on the suicidal. In the backstory, his wife has died and he reaches the stage where he actually puts a gun to his head and is only moments away from killing himself. He's lost his family. That's his need. As you watch the movie, you see the relationship between Gibson's Riggs and his partner develop to the point where Murtaugh and his family essentially adopt Riggs into the family. By the end of the film, the two have caught the bad guys and eat Christmas dinner together. Riggs has filled that hole and found himself a family.

• **The Tempest:** At the end of Shakespeare's play, the wizard Prospero has wreaked revenge on his enemies, regained his stolen kingdom, and found a husband for his daughter, Miranda. But to regain his lost life and riches, he must forever give up magic and supernatural powers. That is the decision he makes, the price for successfully achieving his goals.

The great French film director Jean Renoir (son of the famous painter) once said: "Learning is being able to see the relationship between things."

It is, in my opinion, a profound statement that bears a lot of thinking about, particularly in regard to storytelling. An understanding of dramatic structure is important, not because it is a pattern you should follow slavishly, but because it is a tool that helps you construct your story and build relationships in an emotionally powerful and satisfying way. It is a starting point for creativity, not an end in itself.

As an exercise, list an inventory of your skills as a writer—and as a storyteller. What are your strengths? What are your weaknesses? What do you do well? Create characters? Write strong atmospheric description or snappy dialogue? What would you like to strengthen? What are your weak points? Clichéd plotting? Scenes that seem to have no real life or zing?

Be honest. This is for nobody else's eyes but your own. Try to identify what is driving you to be a writer of stories, what you expect to get out of the experience. What compels you against all odds to do this thing called "writing" for a living?

## EXERCISES

1. Next time you watch a movie, study it carefully for the plot points we've discussed. Examine it for structure, for why things happen the way they do. Nothing (hardly ever, anyway) is by chance in a finished screenplay. *The Fugitive* is a wonderful example of strong dramatic structure.

2. Once you've done that, reread the last book you read. This time, read it with a pencil in hand and mark the plot points. After you've done this with about fifty books and films, you'll be writing plots like a pro.

3. Come up with five "What if . . ." or "Suppose . . ." ideas each week. Then pick one each month and start asking—and answering—the question "Why" about this idea. Then write a complete synopsis, detailing the beginning, middle, and end of your story.

*Chapter Five*

# Characters

This is, perhaps, the most important chapter in this book. Plot is what characters do next, and characters are the hub of all narrative work. So almost all narrative structural problems can be fixed with solutions that involve rethinking and reworking characters and characterization.

When in trouble, in other words, rethink and rework your characters until the problem is solved, and your book will start to feel as though it's writing itself. This, of course, is a lot easier said than done. But it is, at least, a plan of action and a way of attacking narrative problems when they inevitably arise.

## THE STORY IS *WHO* IT HAPPENS TO

Here's a basic thing to remember: The story is *not* what happens; the story is *who* it happens to.

We read narrative fiction and nonfiction to visit new worlds and become involved in the lives of interesting people. Fiction, in particular, these days is also concerned with extremes—emotional traumas, watershed moments in a character's life, moral and ethical dilemmas, and so forth.

In nearly all cases, problems with plotting and general problems that writers characterize (excuse the pun!) as a book "not working" stem from a need to rethink qualities they have—or have not—given their characters.

Consider the example of a woman amateur sleuth who is in too restrictive a marriage to investigate a crime effectively.

"But I've created terrific conflict with her domineering husband," I hear you say.

Unfortunately, it doesn't help in the creation of your story if the conflict you've created, however powerful, causes your primary character to be either reactive or passive. This is particularly true if she is the heroine of a mystery in which she is expected to actively ferret out clues and expose the guilty. If she is merely reacting to things the bad guys do to her all the time, or she stumbles across clues or a solution by luck or coincidence, your story will be weak and emotionally bland.

Suppose you plot a story wherein the amateur sleuth sees a crime, takes a picture of it and then exhibits the picture. The villain sees the picture and comes after your heroine fearing she is about to expose him.

The problem here is that your heroine has done nothing to cause the villain to be brought to justice. It could be argued that she has exhibited a picture, but in reality, he has initiated all the running here, not her.

However, if she takes definite and increasingly life-endangering steps in order to flush him out of his secure place, she is a positive character.

If everything revolves around your story's antagonist panicking enough to go after her, you have a structural flaw in the story that is best solved by rethinking the qualities of the heroine. Give her more spunk, even if she is frightened while doing whatever it is she does, and more decisiveness, and you have someone with whom readers want to spend some time, and about whom they begin to care. She has to act *despite* her domineering husband, not because of his whims and wishes.

## PLOT IS WHAT CHARACTERS DO NEXT

Character is plot (which is another way of saying plot is what characters do next). This means that your story is the interaction of a character's specific personality with a set of—usually—external circumstances. What makes your story interesting is that the events of the story unfold in a way that is unique to that particular character and who she is, and the solution is usually drawn from the unique qualities the character possesses or develops as the story moves to its climax. If the same things happened to a different character, those events, just as in real life, would happen in a different way. That means that when a story isn't working for some reason, say the pacing is off or the viewpoint doesn't work, the structural storytelling problems can be reduced to thinking further, or reconsidering your preconceptions of who these characters are and how they relate to each other. For example: Can you combine two characters into one? Should this character have crossed the path of that character in the backstory?

The key to storytelling is conceptualizing what you want to say and then getting an outline or synopsis of that concept on paper. Not an easy task by any means. In fact, developing an initial synopsis of the story may be the hardest job the novelist, in particular, has to do.

## KNOW YOUR CHARACTERS

Take a moment to reread and think about that last paragraph. That simple concept is the key to fixing structural problems in your manuscript.

When in doubt—or in trouble, technically—rethink not only what your characters do, but also who they are. The most powerful stories, dramatically and emotionally, are those that explore circumstances that develop and exploit a character's obsession: What exactly will she do to achieve the goal of this obsession? Just how far will she go?

It took me many years to realize that the essence of what I was doing for students and authors, in terms of fixing structural problems with storytelling, could be reduced for the most part to solving problems relating to character and character relationships.

If you replace your main character with another, the new character would act in a different way to the same set of problems, and the story would unfold differently. If the story unfolds differently, you have to rethink events and outcomes, and that means passive, dull characters can become active, involving people we care about and so forth.

## OUTSIDE CHARACTER, INSIDE CHARACTER

Think of characterization in two ways:

1. There is outer characterization, that is, everything readers can observe about a character: how she speaks, how she dresses, what she wears for one type of meeting and what she wears for another, body language, and so forth.

2. And there is deep character, that is, the emotional and psychological parts of the character that are revealed under the pressure of the story. Readers wouldn't—and shouldn't—know about this inner life unless the events of the story bring it out.

Here are two examples: A rich man finds a wallet. The rich man looks inside, notes a few credit cards and one thousand dollars in cash, searches for some sign of who the wallet belongs to, shrugs, and returns it, intact, to its owner. He did the expected thing, and readers share his pleasure in allowing his sense of honor and honesty to come to the fore.

What if, instead, a poor man finds the wallet? This guy is out of work and living in a homeless shelter. His family is hungry, but he returns the wallet anyway.

There's nothing smug or self-satisfying about this guy. Both he and the rich guy have done the honorable thing, but while readers can admire the rich guy's honesty, they are not particularly emotionally involved in his story or his decision. They are, however, involved in the poor guy's decision, because it will cost him, perhaps dearly. The author has ratcheted up the emotional stakes of the story. Readers know this is a man for whom the right things, principles, are important, and they can admire his act, knowing it could not have been easy. His decision to return the wallet reveals a great deal about his inner character.

Now, a rich man who *keeps* the wallet also reveals something about his character. That, too, will involve readers' emotions in some fashion. So good structure, at its core, can be thought of as placing strongly drawn characters in circumstances that will create the most intense drama, that is, the most conflict and emotional impact.

Dustin Hoffman reveals deep character in *Tootsie* when he decides to take off the dress on national TV and give up being Dorothy Michaels. In Charles Dickens's *A Tale of Two Cities*, deep character is what Sydney Carlton reveals when he goes to the guillotine in place of the husband of the woman he loves, saying, "It is a far, far better thing that I do, than I have ever done; it is a far, far better rest that I go to, than I have ever known."

You can't change deep-character qualities without completely altering the story, and thus the way it should be put together.

If you've written a story about a guy who finds the wallet and returns it and a movie producer comes along and says, "I love your story, but let's make it a woman, let's make her black, let's put her in India, and let's dress her a certain way," you can do all those things and end up with a different *kind* of story, but something that is still *in essence* the original idea as long as the characters share personality traits. However, if the producer says, "Let's make her a woman who wouldn't return the wallet," he's just changed your story radically.

Deep character is concerned with *why* people do what they do, by *showing* that inner element in a dramatic way, rather than *telling* us that so-and-so was an honest man or a dishonest one. It is that part of character you cannot change without changing your plot.

The father of psychoanalysis, Sigmund Freud, said that only by owning up to our true desires, realizing it is our appetites that pull us to dark and curious stuff, such as stories of satanic worship or UFOs, can we attain self-knowledge. This must also be true of your characters, of course, and the inner engines that drive them to do whatever it is they must do in your narratives. If a desire is bottled up for too long, stimulated continually but unrecognized or repressed, Freud reckons there's a strong chance it will manifest itself in some fashion in sudden and unexpected acts. Something violent may come of suppression and disavowal as appetites grow and the self-consciousness needed to control these appetites fades away or is "Prozaced" out of existence. To know your desires, and those of your characters, is to be able to exert greater sway over them.

If your plot is in trouble in some way, reconsidering one or other—or both—of these character elements is going to change the structure of your narrative in a substantial enough way that it will allow you to take a fresh look at whether you are recounting your story as effectively as you could. And more to the point, with the right change, you increase the emotional power of the narrative, that is, increase its "grabbing" quality and thus your chances of getting published.

## CHARACTER AND CONFLICT

Your characters can only be as interesting as the forces arrayed against them. By that, I mean that a character reveals himself by rising to the level necessary to overcome the conflict.

Consider the character Rocky. Most people forget that in the first movie he doesn't win the big fight at its climax. The path of the character and the story is such that this doesn't really matter. It is the journey Rocky makes that is important. In the first movie in particular, but also in the subsequent ones to a lesser degree, if Rocky was presented as a guy who rose to the level of heavyweight boxing contender by overcoming a parade of patsies, guys who fell over if you tapped them on the chin, what would you have learned about his depth of character, his dedication, his perseverance?

The answer is, not much. If the people and problems defeated were easily overcome, the story would be neither emotionally involving nor of enough dramatic interest to bother following Rocky's rise to the level of a world heavyweight championship boxer. How do you show great tenacity and strength of character, but by dramatizing strength of will in some fashion. Doing so gives you a basis for inventing incidental and secondary characters who will help you discover these elements in your hero as you watch him rise to fame.

*Rocky* works because the character is continually placing himself in increasingly challenging and difficult situations that he eventually overcomes. So, your opposition has got to be as dynamic as your protagonist.

It's also important you see your characters from their own points of view.

By that, I mean, don't write your villains so that they come across as moustache-twirling psychotics. Alice Orr, an agent and author, as well as a terrific teacher, put it best I think: "A villain is still the hero of his own story."

Someone once asked the actor Lee Marvin about playing bad guys for most of his career. Marvin said, "What bad guys? I didn't play any bad guys. I just played guys who were getting through life the way they knew best."

His point was that inside their own heads, "villains" don't think of themselves that way, and they're more interesting people because of it.

Try this exercise: Write two or three paragraphs from the point of view of each of your characters from your book. You'll have all of your characters sort of justifying their behavior: "I am Adolph Hitler, and I'm really a pretty good guy once you get to know me. Children call me Uncle Wolfie and like to sit on my knee."

## LET YOUR CHARACTERS BE THEMSELVES

In your stories, whether they are fictional or re-creations of real events, it's important your characters act out of their own natures, rather than be manipulated by the demands of a plot. This is a common mistake with beginning writers. They want something "exciting" or "important" plotwise to happen in their stories, and regardless of the kind of characters they have invented to populate their fictive worlds, these authors are going to make this excitement happen. An absurd example of what I'm talking about would be to cast Huckleberry Finn as the lead character in William Goldman's *Marathon Man*.

Sometimes a writer gets to a point in the plot when he

needs something to happen and he just has the character do it. The reader, though, instinctively senses that something is wrong. It's just a little too convenient, a little too contrived. That's because the character has acted in contradiction to her nature.

One of the classic examples of this kind of problem is in the old John Wayne movie *Stagecoach*. It's about a group of people traveling in the Old West in a stagecoach. They are attacked by Arapaho as they are crossing the plains and have to take refuge in a way station. Most of the film is about the personal conflicts of the passengers under the stress of imminent danger from the threatening hostiles just outside the walls of the way station. It's a great movie.

Only one problem: Traditionally, when the Native Americans attacked a stagecoach, they would shoot the lead horses in the team pulling the coach. The horses in the rest of the team would stumble, and before you knew it, the coach would either stop cold or overturn and crash. Either way, the hostiles then made short work of the passengers. But the writers wouldn't have had a story had they done that. So they ignored the problem, and as a result made the Native Americans look stupid. Luckily, this was a movie about the characters' relationships with each other, rather than about the Native Americans, but it's a classic example of plot taking precedence over logic or character truth.

Here's another example of what I mean. A student of Gary's wrote a story about two men who come over to her house. One of the men is a pretty timid sort, and yet, out of the blue, he volunteers to help find her missing brother. The question immediately becomes how come all of a sudden he's brave enough to volunteer to go off and look for this missing brother? What's his motivation? The answer is, of course, that the author needed him to do that and didn't bother to establish any kind of credible motivation. The character's actions just weren't real.

So the author and Gary brainstormed a little, and they realized that the problem with the story was that the character was acting against his own nature. The solution was to go back and create a situation where the character is hoping to meet a potential wife or girlfriend, and when he's visiting this woman, he's struck by a vision of her as a potential mate.

Now, when he volunteers to look for the brother, readers know, without necessarily being told, that he's thinking, *Gee, you know if I go looking for the brother, I'll have to come over and visit this house a lot and maybe I'll see this beautiful woman again, and maybe we'll get closer and become friends, and then lovers and then . . .* So, of course, he agrees to do it, and he's acting against his own timid nature but for a credible reason. But more importantly, by taking a weakness and working on making it a strength, he becomes a more interesting character. He wants to be around to see this woman again, so he's overcoming inner demons and flaws to achieve his goal. That's the point.

Make sure the character's doing something *he* wants to do, not just something *you* want him to do. Listen to what your characters tell you, particularly the good guys who do bad things and the sick and twisted psychotics who stalk through your stories.

Characters have to decide their own fates. Nobody wants to read a story about a woman who's on a ship and there's a storm and she falls overboard with just a small dinghy, and for six days she's in the dinghy working her way to shore, and there are fifteen-foot waves and heavy winds and rain, and she's starving, and she gets six miles from shore and some marine captain comes along and plucks her out of the ocean. That's not good storytelling.

You don't want someone coming in at the last moment and helping your character out. The fun of reading is to enjoy the emotional roller coaster of the character's experiences during the story and to admire the grace with which characters use their wiles and wit to solve the problems that beset them. So make sure your character is in charge of her own fate, that it's not taken care of for her.

## MELODRAMA

The word *melodrama* is one you've probably heard, and it's worth talking about in characterization. Melodrama is often defined as characters overreacting to what's going on.

A lot of times, writers make the mistake of looking at something they've written, realize that it's melodramatic and cut back on the big scene by diminishing its emotional potential. They suffer what amounts to a sort of loss of creative nerve at the last moment.

But there's a way to fix this kind of structural problem.

Let's say the situation is this: A young girl comes home at two in the morning. The mother is waiting up for her. When the girl comes home, the mother just goes crazy, screaming, crying, throwing things, and shouting, "What are you doing home so late?" The reader looks at this and thinks, *Wow, this is kind of over the top. Why is the mother overreacting?* Your tendency may be to rewrite the scene and play it all down. But what if you try another approach instead?

Looked at more closely, melodrama is not really about characters overreacting; it's about characters having no appropriate motivation for their behavior, and thus they become caricatures of emotion. The problem is not the reaction but that the character is undermotivated.

If you want to hold that big scene and reap the rewards of readers' continuing loyalty by giving them a gripping experience, you want to keep a lot of those emotional fireworks. What you need to do is foreshadow the character's reaction in the scene by thinking about a better motivation for her behavior than just the girl arriving home late from a date.

In this case, it might be that the mother had an older daughter who died in an automobile accident at two in the morning six months before. All the memories are still fresh and raw. The surviving daughter stays out late, and the mother's memories of that tragedy build up. When the daughter comes home late, the mother explodes. The solution is to raise—or clarify—the motivation, rather than lower the emotional temperature.

The biggest structural problems can be reduced to coming

up with believable answers to the question *why*, especially when it concerns a character's behavior. And now we've come back to characters being plot again.

## THE SUN AND ITS PLANETS

Your main character can be thought of as the sun of your fictional universe.

Picture this sun with all these planets, the minor characters of your story, orbiting around it. These minor characters are vehicles for the progression of the narrative story lines, but they should also reflect varying aspects of your main character's personality.

Let's say you have a character named Dennis. Dennis may have a number of character traits. Suppose you make him antagonistic, bashful, cunning, and desperate. In your book, he's going to be revealed via a number of minor characters whose structural role in the book is going to include reflecting these qualities.

Dennis is antagonistic: You'll show this through his relationship with his boss, someone Dennis doesn't get along with. To reinforce this, you can develop a subplot about whether Dennis is going to lose his job.

He's bashful: He meets nurse June. He'd like to go out with her, but he's afraid to call her.

He's cunning: He figures out that his sister-in-law Carol knows June, and he gets Carol to find out if June likes him enough to go out with him.

Dennis is also desperate: He's bet every cent he has on a horse, Biscuits for Dinner, and this desperation is reflected in the character Louie, who is Dennis's bookie.

The broader point here is that ideally *everything* in your novel should have a purpose for being there, including the minor characters who come on stage to give the main character a clue or point the way ahead. Narrative is a very considered art form, and it is reflective of real life only in the sense that what we read should be credible, believable. So spear carriers should have a function besides being eccentrics, objects of humor or thrills, or just people you've discovered you like whom you want to include in your story.

## PICK AND CHOOSE

While you try as much as possible to plan and develop a character in all the variety of his personality, you may end up using only little clusters of that information as it relates to the story you're developing.

I'll give you an example. A real person might play golf, listen to rock and roll, enjoy basketball, read *Moby Dick*, eat Thai food, and take part in amateur ballet dancing. That may seem too much, or at least contradictory, and have no real shape or direction, but few of us have distinct patterns in our lives except in hindsight.

However, when you write that character, readers only need to know what is necessary for the telling of that story. The rule of thumb is: If it is an important enough character detail for readers to know, it is important enough to dramatize.

Mark Twain once said: "Don't tell me there was a little old lady. Bring the old bag out on the stage and let me see her." That was his not so subtle way of saying, show, don't tell, your characters.

Bring your character onto the stage and let the reader see who she is and how she feels by how she acts when alone and with others, not by what she says or thinks.

## VIEWPOINT

Character has two other structural jobs in the narrative: It is the deciding factor for a writer's choice of which viewpoint to use to tell the story, and how many, and it gives description a function in the narrative that is more than just words setting a scene.

It's important to remember that when you were in school you learned in English that first person is I, and second person is *you*, and third person is *he* or *she* or *it*. This is not to be confused with viewpoint. When I say something is in a person's viewpoint, it means that for a least that part of the book that character is telling the story in some fashion.

Try this exercise. It's *very hard*, so you'll need to really concentrate. You're going to describe a house. It can be any house, it doesn't matter. There are rules to this exercise about how you describe your house, however:

- You can't imagine it and describe it from the front
- You can't describe it from the back
- You can't describe it from either the left side or the right side
- You can't describe it from above looking down
- You can't describe it from the basement looking up
- You can't describe it from inside.

In fact, you're not any place in reference to that house. So how do you imagine it and describe it? Is this an impossible exercise? Of course it is! You can't picture the house—or anything else—this way. It can't be done. Why? Because you have no frame of reference.

We call that frame of reference viewpoint.

In order to really grasp the concept of viewpoint, try thinking of it as if it were a matter of camera placement. You're going to see later that it's not quite that simple, but it's a good place to start.

In the narrative, your reader has got to *be* somewhere in reference to everything you write in order to understand and experience your story. What's more, to maximize the emotional content of the book, you should establish this viewpoint from the outset of the story. Like the exercise with the house, if you don't start out with clues as to whose eyes readers are looking through or whose shoulder they're looking over, the description will sit like a lump in gravy and the book will lack emotional punch.

Try this exercise. (I promise you this one is a real exercise. No more tricks.) Write no more than one page for each of the following four descriptions:

A baby lies in a crib in a nursery. Choose the child's age and any other details you wish, such as whether the baby is in a home or in a hospital. It's all completely up to you. Just describe the room.

However, do not mention the child or his feelings or any emotional state or thoughts at all. Stick to pure visual description and choice of detail to do this exercise. You are almost a camera, although you do have the power of metaphor and simile to draw upon as long as you don't overuse it.

Now, describe the same scene from the point of view of a doting father peeping in. Again, don't mention the father or his feelings.

Describe the scene a third time, this time from the point of view of a terrified mother. No mention of her and her fears.

Finally, describe the same scene from the child's point of view.

## Character, Viewpoint, and Description

I hope you notice that the first part of that exercise affords a description that is generic when compared to those that follow. It is a lot like the exercise with the house without a viewpoint. The viewpoint in that first description ends up being the writer's.

Now, unless you're going to write a story in which the author is allowed to talk to the reader, a nineteenth-century technique that's rarely used today, it should become obvious that description is a function of viewpoint, and viewpoint is the end result of knowing something about who is doing the observing. So both viewpoint and description are extensions of character. If that is the case, then description is a function of character and the same visual image will vary depending on who is doing the seeing.

Inexperienced storytellers, when they write, though interestingly enough not when they verbally tell stories, place the readers in a certain position in regard to the viewpoint of the story and then suddenly yank them into another viewpoint at an inappropriate moment, such as in the middle of the scene.

Here's an example:

> In the rattling subway car, Gordon felt somehow co-
> cooned from the bitterness of the outside world, at least
> for a while. If you sat long enough, and Gordon had
> nothing but time on his hands until tonight, you could
> observe the flow of passengers on and off the subway
> car. Hunched in a corner, studiously avoided by the
> New Yorkers who turned their backs to him whenever
> possible, Gordon began to feel not only that he was in-
> visible, but that he was irrelevant. Mary was determined
> not to make contact with anyone on the train. Keep
> your attention on your Bible passage and just make sure
> you don't make eye contact with anyone, particularly
> men, she thought. The difficulty was that the bum in a
> corner seat a few feet from where she stood by the door
> stank to high heaven and kept staring at her and then
> ducking away.

So who is doing the observing here? Is it Gordon, or is it
Mary? What happens when they eventually have to interact?
Whose viewpoint will the writer choose? He can't swing back
and forth giving each viewpoint every time one of them speaks
or thinks because readers will get nauseous from the violent
changes in camera angle. They will also have no touchstone
with which to decide whom to identify with in a scene, and
thus the writer will rob the scene of any potential emotional
impact. He must pick a viewpoint and stay with it within a
scene. If you want a more detailed explanation of viewpoint,
take a look at my book *The Elements of Storytelling* (John
Wiley & Sons).

## Try to Keep to One Viewpoint

In order to maximize the emotional impact of your narrative,
you should use as few viewpoints as possible to tell your story.
Over the shoulder or through the eyes and in the head of *one*
character is ideal from a perspective of maximum emotional
impact. It's not always possible to do that, however. The

reader cares about one or two people, but if she starts living vicariously and intimately through the eyes of too many characters and viewpoints, she becomes bewildered, forced to put the narrative at arm's length in order to process the story, which is the exact opposite of what you should want from a reader.

We can think of viewpoint as being of several types: omniscient, minor character, major character, and multiple.

## Omniscient Viewpoint

Omniscient viewpoint is what is called the God view. It means you can know anything. You can know about other places, other times, future and past:

> Humpty Dumpty didn't realize it, but soon he would have a great fall, and all the King's horses and all the King's men would not be able to put him together again.

Well, if Humpty didn't realize what was happening, then, of course, you're not in Humpty's viewpoint. You're in a godlike viewpoint that knows what's going to happen in the future and the past and what's going on in Toledo, Ohio, and anywhere else.

This is called omniscience. It's not something you should use. It's not even in style these days. It was big in the nineteenth century. "Listen, dear reader, while I tell you about these people," sort of thing. You shouldn't use this viewpoint for two reasons: First, it's very difficult to do effectively because you have too many options:

> Jack and Jill went up the hill to fetch a pail of water. Jack fell down . . .

OK, now what? Do I stay in Jack's point of view and go down the hill and see what it feels like to tumble down a hill? Or do I stay with Jill and watch Jack fall down the hill? And when Jill goes tumbling after, what do I do? Do I get inside Jill's head and describe what it feels like to go tumbling after?

Or do I switch to Jack and look up the hill at Jill coming down the hill? There are too many options. It becomes unwieldy.

Second, and more importantly, it's not really the way we experience life. We don't know what's going to happen a half hour from now or two years from now. We don't know what's going on in Toledo, Ohio. We probably don't need to know, either. Because we don't experience life that way, the omniscient viewpoint runs against the grain of the reader's everyday experience. The best advice is don't use it except for comedic effect.

## Minor-Character Viewpoint

What do I mean by this?

Consider this opening line: "Call me Ishmael." Readers are about to enter the world of *Moby Dick*, through the eyes of a secondary character. Ishmael is going to tell the story of Captain Ahab and his obsessive quest to destroy the great white whale.

A more widely read example is probably Dr. John Watson. Who? The guy who tells us all about the exploits of his close friend, Sherlock Holmes. All the Sherlock Holmes stories, you may recall, are told from the viewpoint of Dr. Watson. Think about why that's true and you'll get a real understanding about what this kind of viewpoint in particular, but viewpoint in general, is all about.

Here's a typical statement Watson might make in the middle of a Sherlock Holmes story:

> Holmes picked up the coffee cup and he sniffed it. A strange look came into his eyes.

That's all Watson knows. Holmes doesn't say anything. The cup goes back, and at the end of the story, Holmes solves the crime:

> When I sniffed the cup I smelled this very rare brand of cognac, which I discovered only comes from South Africa, so it must have been Colonel Garon who did the

murder because he was only newly arrived from Cape Town.

Watson finds out and the readers find out at the same time. If the Sherlock Holmes stories were written from Holmes's point of view, you'd have a different situation:

> Sherlock picked up the coffee cup and sniffed. Immediately he knew. The odor was unmistakable. "Call Inspector Lestrade," he told Watson. "We have our murderer. He will need to arrest Garon before he leaves for the night train to Paris."
>
> "My dear Holmes, are you mad?" Watson said. There was hint of annoyance with his friend in his tone. "You haven't been indulging again in that appalling cocaine addiction of yours, have you?"
>
> Holmes turned his famous profile to Watson and the coldness of his gaze and the firm set of his jaw announced *that* topic would be discussed no further. "Cognac, my dear doctor. Here, smell for yourself, the odor is unmistakable. South African Cognac." With a dismissive gesture of one hand he announced, "This case is closed. It is of no more interest to me."

We've just defanged the drama and the climax of this story because of a poor choice of viewpoint. The reader feels, and correctly, that she's entitled to all the information that comes to the viewpoint character. And so Sir Arthur Conan Doyle doesn't use Sherlock Holmes's viewpoint because Conan Doyle wants to save this revelation for later and maximize the drama at the same time.

That is what viewpoint is all about.

Viewpoint is about how best to reveal information, who has that information and how you want to give it to the reader.

## Major-Character Viewpoint
Let's talk about a single, major-character viewpoint. This should be what you use most in your narratives. It means you

have chosen a character and thus a viewpoint for your narrative and everything that character knows is available to the reader.

However, the reader can know everything she knows *only* when she knows it, no sooner or later, no more and no less.

Let's assume the viewpoint character's name is Gary. You can write about Gary and what he knows about a situation:

> Gary walked into the room. The carpet was green.
> There were five or six writers waiting to hear him say
> something brilliant. He had on a copper shirt.

All of these are things Gary is aware of. And you can't add things that violate the reader's sense of what makes logical sense in the narrative:

> At that very moment some looney psycho by the
> name of Virgil Strunk crept up behind Gary. "I'm going
> to get that writing teacher person," Virgil thought.

The reason, of course, is that you've stepped out of Gary's viewpoint. You have jerked the reader around to another direction without warning.

## Multiple Viewpoint

This leads us to a discussion of multiple viewpoints. This just means that you use a number of different viewpoints in your novel. It's not omniscient, though, because at any given point in the novel, readers only have access to one character's thoughts and feelings.

There are a couple of things to remember about this. First of all, don't use a lot of viewpoints just for the heck of it. Very often beginning writers—and some professionals, too—use multiple viewpoints as a crutch to avoid developing one character with depth and because the writer forgets that the story is not *what happens*, but *whom it happens to*. So, in order to tell his story, and because he's having trouble figuring out how to give all the relevant information to readers, the writer slides into lots of viewpoints, rather than trying to explore the problems that arise from learning about a single character's life and emotions and the moral and ethical problems the story raises about that character's life.

It's OK to use multiple viewpoints, but they work best in bigger, more epic kinds of narratives or in the reconstruction of specific events in, say, a true crime piece. Usually, it's best not to use more than three or four viewpoints. The important thing to keep in mind is that the more viewpoints you use, the less intimacy you give the reader with any one of these characters.

The key to successfully switching between multiple viewpoints is to do it at logical times in the narrative. Do it between chapters, certainly between scenes, but don't change viewpoint characters *in* a scene. If you do, it will have that quality of yanking the reader around. Also, once you've decided to change viewpoint, at the start of the book you need to announce to readers in some fashion that one of the rules of this book is that they can now have John's viewpoint as well as Mary's. If you decide to do this, however, you better use both points of view.

If, for example, the bulk of the book is written in Mary's viewpoint and only chapter two is in John's viewpoint, the book will feel out of whack. It's going to feel to the reader as if you have changed viewpoint once to solve some technical story problem. So use multiple viewpoint if you need to, but limit it to two, three or, at the most, four viewpoints, not every single character in a book. And keep it consistent until the end of the narrative.

## Choosing Viewpoint

How do you choose a viewpoint? Most of the time you'll know which to use. In the planning of and the advance thinking about your story, it becomes obvious that this is Marvin's story or Janet's story.

But there are other times when a story comes to you and you can think of two or three different ways to tell it, two or three different character viewpoints you could use, and you have to decide which one is best.

Here's the guiding principle I stated before that will work with *any* narrative writing question: All major problems with narrative storytelling have a structural basis. The solution is always to rethink, or otherwise examine and modify the characters who are populating your story.

The basis for deciding the best way to do that—or anything else in writing a narrative—is to filter your choices through the lens of emotional power.

Ask yourself, What will give my story the most emotional impact? What will dilute this emotional power?

Choose the solution that pumps up the emotional power of the narrative and you will never go far wrong. Emotional power grabs the reader by the throat and doesn't let go until the last word of the last sentence of the last page.

When in doubt, go for the throat—metaphorically, of course!

Here are couple of other things to consider.

Who is the active character in your story? Remember, earlier we talked about good ideas, and good ideas are about characters who are not reactive or passive. Who is the character who really *does* something in this story? Who really takes action, takes control of his fate and perhaps the fate of others? He makes a good viewpoint character. Certainly, books have been written about people who were passive, who sort of experienced the story secondhand, but those stories are difficult to write and they're not very satisfying to read.

Finally, of course, who is the person who has the information that you want to reveal to the reader and in the order that you want to reveal it? He may well be the best viewpoint character. In the case of Sherlock Holmes, for example, Watson certainly is. He has the information in the order Conan Doyle wants the reader to get it. Watson, like us, finds out at the end of the story who committed the murder, whereas Sherlock Holmes often realizes who the murderer is halfway through the story.

## The Deeper Meaning of Viewpoint

Let's talk for a moment about character and the deeper meaning of viewpoint.

For the sake of discussion, and simplicity, we've been treating viewpoint as a sort of camera placement. In reality, it's more than that.

When you choose the viewpoint, you choose how the reader is going to experience that story. You filter the narrative through the viewpoint character's eyes and ears, feelings and emotions. The story is shaped and determined in large part by that character's perceptions of life. When you change the viewpoint, you alter the language, attitude, everything about how the story is being told. This is why changing viewpoints unexpectedly is so disconcerting to the reader and is such poor narrative technique.

## EXERCISES

1. Think of the most villainous, nasty, rotten, miserable person you can—someone really awful. Write three to five paragraphs about this person, in first person, to convey what he thinks of himself.

2. Write a scene with two people in it. First, write it from the point of view of character A. Then, write it from character B's point of view. Write it in third person. Rewrite the same scene with two different characters. Again, write from each viewpoint.

*Chapter Six*

# Goals

W e're going to talk goals: why you're putting together the elements of your story the way you are and how best to focus and structure the pieces of your story so it is smooth and seamless.

To begin, let's talk about tennis.

Tennis is a sport with an ultimate goal: You have to win more sets than your opponent. You can win by beating your opponent two sets out of three or three sets out of five or whatever you agree on ahead of time. Tennis also has what you might call intermediary goals: To win a set you have to be the first player to win a certain number of games, usually six. And tennis has minor goals: To win a game, you have to be the first to get four points; and to win a point, you have to hit the ball over the net, past your opponent. All these progressive goals in a tennis match make sense, because you understand that the ultimate goal is to outwit your opponent and win the game. What's more, each progressive goal lends drama to the game in a mounting sequence that builds one upon another.

But what would happen if you had a tennis match in which the players just hit balls back and forth but didn't bother to keep any kind of score? Where's the drama, beyond the immediacy of individual rallies across the net? Where are the tie-breakers, the cliff-hangers, the unison "oohs" and "ahs" of the crowd as rallies of shots become increasingly hard to return, each shot retrieved with ever more amazing displays of athletic prowess and technical skill.

If no one knew what the players were trying to accomplish, it would be impossible to keep score. The game would lack drama and make no sense. And if you didn't keep score, you wouldn't bother to stay long at a tennis match, because there wouldn't be an ultimate goal—a winner.

The same thing is true with your story.

If the readers don't understand what your character is trying to achieve, they don't know whether your character's gotten closer to her goal or farther away from it.

Readers don't know how to keep score.

## HOW TO KEEP SCORE

Throughout your book there should be a series of goals: There's an ultimate goal, intermediate goals, and minor goals.

Let's look at a science fiction novel as an example, but it could just as easily be a piece of narrative nonfiction.

In *Planet of the Apes* (aka *Monkey Planet*), by Pierre Boulle, the ultimate goal is for the stranded astronaut to get back to Earth. The intermediate goal is for him to find and steal a spaceship. The minor goal is for him to escape from the apes who have captured him and may well enslave him for the rest of his life if they don't kill him and stuff him in a museum, as they did his partners.

All the events in the story hold the reader's interest because they are linked by goals—the reader understands how the hero, achieving each lesser goal, is led to his ultimate goal. If the reader didn't know what that ultimate goal was, the scenes would just be boring and disconnected and wouldn't mean anything.

## GOALS IN THE SCENE

Sometimes a scene that isn't working can be fixed easily by putting the goal in the right place. Here's an example. It is the kind of thing writers of narrative nonfiction have to tackle.

Let's treat this example as though it were a piece of nonfiction. You've done the research and spoken to the principal

characters and witnesses, so you know all of the events, however trivial, actually happened. The reason you're writing a
book about two boys is that they will ultimately get together
to murder their parents. You are reconstructing for the reader
the days and hours the boys spent together before the crime.

Here's the scene as it's originally written: There are two
teenage boys, Bobby and Timmy. Timmy is the younger
brother and shares a room with Bobby.

One night Timmy stays out late. He comes home, walks in
the front door, walks up the stairs, walks into the bedroom,
slowly undresses, and gets into bed. At the end of the scene,
you write a paragraph that says, "Timmy was glad that Bobby
hadn't woken up, because he would have been mad at him
for staying out late and would have started punching him."

The problem is, readers don't understand what the point
of this particular scene is. What was Timmy's goal?

Now, let's turn the structure of the scene around.

Take the last sentence, "Timmy was glad that Bobby hadn't
woken up, because he would have been mad at him for staying
out late and would have started punching him."

Rewrite it to read something like, "Timmy hoped his
brother Bobby wouldn't wake up and beat him up for coming
home late." Put this sentence pretty close to the beginning of
the scene.

Now, readers view the scene quite differently.

Look how much more interested the reader is in what is
going to happen as Timmy slips the key in the lock, as he
climbs the creaking stairs and makes what seem to be intolera-
bly loud noises. Will they wake Bobby? Timmy reaches the
bedroom. He opens the door and stumbles in the dark. Bobby
turns over. Has Timmy woken him? Will Bobby give him a
beating after all? Painstakingly quietly Timmy undresses. The
loud rustling as he unfastens buttons, the noise of metal zip-
pers unpeeling—are these going to disturb his brother?

Timmy walks across the floor to the bed. Does the floor
creak? Does he trip over something unseen in the darkness?
Will Bobby wake up and beat the hell out of him? Timmy

climbs into bed. Ah, this time he's gotten away with it.

By writing the scene this way, you've shown not just the immediate goal of how Timmy evades a beating, but how the scene is a part of the overall goal of the narrative, how Bobby was able to terrorize his younger brother into helping him commit this awful crime.

It's worth recalling that the central question, the goal for most readers of narrative nonfiction, is, How could this event have happened? How could these boys have done this terrible thing?

Now, in your scene, either Bobby wakes up or he doesn't, but readers are compelled to read the scene because they have a question. Timmy has a goal: get into bed without waking Bobby. As a result, readers understood how to keep score. If Bobby awakens, Timmy loses the tennis match. If Bobby stays asleep, Timmy wins. Either way, it all becomes more compelling.

## THE NARRATIVE QUESTION

Remember, we're talking about structure, about *how* things are put together.

Throughout your book your characters have a steady stream of goals. At any given point in your narrative, there's something they want. It may be a big thing; it may be a small thing. That goal becomes what Gary called "the narrative question."

The narrative question throughout your book is usually, "Will he get this? Will she get that? Will they ever get what they want?"

Try this tip to strengthen your writing.

Make a sign in large letters to put over your desk. The sign says two things:

*Why?* and

*What does my character want?*

Whenever you're writing, look at that sign and ask yourself those two questions. Then you will understand not only what your character will do next, but also some kind of motivation for that action.

You'll know how to keep score in your story and what your character is trying to achieve.

## TYPES OF GOALS

Goals can take a number of forms. A goal in a scene could be an object, such as *he's trying to get the diamonds that she keeps in the safe in the bedroom.*

A goal could be a more abstract idea: *He's trying to get cooperation to put together a deal of some sort to raise money.*

It could be an internal goal: *A character is trying to come to some understanding or knowledge of himself.*

A student of Gary's once wrote a scene in which a character was going along, driving into a city, looking at this place and that, and at the end of the scene, she realizes that her father's death has changed her. Having reached that point, the writer understood she had to go back to the beginning of the scene and plant that as the goal: In this case, the character was trying to come to some new understanding.

The goal for a scene may occur in the scene, or it may be obvious from some previous scene.

Consider the Bobby and Timmy scene. Maybe in a previous scene, when Timmy was hanging out with his girlfriend (the one who will ultimately sit on the witness stand for the prosecution and tell the jury what Timmy confessed to her about his role in this double murder), he said to her, "I'd better be quiet when I get home, because if Bobby hears me he'll beat the crap out of me for being so late."

So now, when Timmy gets home and puts the key in the lock, walks across the creaking floor, etc., readers understand the goal of keeping quiet. You no longer have to write it into the scene at the beginning. If the goal is not clear, of course, then you have to put it in the scene, as we did in our first example of Bobby and Timmy.

A goal can be stated in a lot of ways. It might be a question. Remember the TV show *Twin Peaks*? The question driving it was, Who killed Laura Palmer? The goal was to reveal the murderer.

There are many ways of achieving a goal, and you try to do it in both subtle and graceful ways. Primarily, however, make sure that from the outset of the scene your reader understands how to read the scene, in other words, how to keep score by understanding what the character's goal is in that scene.

## SEEK—AND MAYBE YOU'LL FIND

Writing students used to come up to Gary and say things like, "Gary, I've written a lot of scenes, and it's true they have no goal, but the writing is fantastic. Some of the best I've ever done. I just *can't* cut them out of the book. What can I do?" Does this sound at all familiar?

Gary's answer used to be: "Doesn't matter. You're going to have to throw those scenes away, because a scene without a goal is like a tennis match without points being scored."

The student would look dejected, and Gary would give a little chuckle and add, "But, don't go throwing those scenes away just yet. It may be they have a goal after all, and you just haven't found it yet.

"Tell you how to find out. Here's the situation: You've written a scene, but you don't completely understand what the main character's goal is? When you get to the end of the scene, ask yourself, What does the character have now that he didn't have at the beginning of the scene? and then, How does he feel about that?"

Here's an example of what Gary was talking about.

You write a scene, and at the end of your scene, your hero gets to kiss Jennifer. How does he feel about that? Well, he probably feels pretty good about that. So his goal was to get a kiss from Jennifer.

What if he feels bad about what happened? Then maybe his goal was to break up with Jennifer.

Early on in Gary's last book, *Baffled in Boston*, the hero, Scotty, is talking to a friend about Molly, who died, and how he feels about that. Scotty ends up confessing that he suspects

Molly was murdered. So what was the point? What did Scotty want?

Let Gary tell you the rest of the story:

"That means his goal in the scene was to announce to somebody that he believed Molly had been murdered, and that's exactly what he does in the scene.

"So, by the end of the scene, I understood the goal. Having figured that out, I went back in the second draft of the manuscript, and in the beginning of the scene, I said something like: 'I had gone to the funeral, and I needed to share my secret belief with somebody, but I didn't know who.' "

## EVERYONE WANTS SOMETHING

Keep in mind that all your characters have goals, no matter how obscure the characters may seem. Characters without goals, however minor, disrupt the flow of the narrative, forcing the audience's attention away from what is important.

Here's an example. You're writing a narrative nonfiction account about your mother, Harriet, and the extraordinary life she led. She goes off to Los Angeles to visit her father, a blue-collar immigrant from Poland. They have a huge fight in which each's resentment of the other comes pouring out. She rushes upstairs, packs a suitcase, walks out of the house. There, in front of the house, is a taxi. Harriet takes the taxi to the airport and goes back home to New York City.

Readers say to themselves: "Wait a minute. That seems a little contrived, doesn't it? A taxi, in LA, that just *happens* to be outside the house when Harriet needs it most. What's going on here?"

And the readers would be right. You have jerked them from what John Gardner used to call the "continuous dream" of your narrative. (Gardner was a well-respected novelist and teacher of creative writing whose book *The Art of Fiction* is one of the most thought-provoking books on writing fiction ever published.)

It is contrived that a taxi just happens to be there when it's needed, and it appears contrived because readers don't understand what the taxi driver's goal is. Why is he there? Is there a hidden significance?

Imagine instead that Harriet rushes into the street with her suitcase and realizes it's almost impossible to hail a cab in LA from the street. She finds a telephone and calls for a taxi, which then arrives and takes her to the airport.

Now, there is no problem believing what happened because the audience understands that the taxi driver, as minor as he is in the story (he'll probably never be seen again), has a goal. What is it? To find passengers to transport from one place to another so he can make a living. It all makes sense because readers understand his goal, even though it's implicit in the scene, not explicit.

## BE BLATANT, THEN GET SUBTLE

You may find it useful in your first drafts to be blatant about a scene's goal. Try to state the goal in the first sentence. For example, "Jack wanted to meet Greta Garbo. Even though she was famed for her reclusiveness, every day he would wait in the street outside her Manhattan home, hoping for a chance to introduce himself."

After you write that scene, it's possible you can remove that overt statement and make the scene subtler.

By the time you get to your final draft, your characters will have goals in all of your scenes.

## EXERCISES

1. Go through your book manuscript and choose five scenes. Identify the goal in each scene.

2. If you haven't completed five scenes yet, take five scenes from a published novel and identify the goals.

3. Watch the movies *The Fugitive*, *Thelma and Louise*, *Unforgiven*, and *Tootsie* (or use any movie you like!) and analyze the scenes for their goals.

# Chapter Seven

# Writing in Scenes

Having talked in general about scenes as the basic structural unit and characters needing a goal, let's talk about scenes and goals more specifically.

Writing a book can seem a daunting task. So many pages to fill, so many words to come up with. At times it can seem as though you're faced with a huge brick wall, impossible to climb over.

But a book is really a cumulative thing. Bit by bit, piece by piece, scene by scene, it all comes together, sometimes before you're even completely aware of what is happening. If you write one page a day, every day for a year, you'll end up with 365 pages—a book-length manuscript. Suddenly, that image of a huge wall fades away and is replaced by a far less daunting image, one of a house being constructed a piece at a time. And the "bricks" that build your "house" are not chapters, but scenes.

## THINKING IN SCENES

Structurally, a chapter can be one scene or several scenes, and the scene can be two pages long or twenty pages long. There is no definite length for either. Broadly, the scene should begin as close to the "meat" of the action in the scene as possible; and it should end when that action has concluded. Write as little setup, explanation, description, etc., as possible:

**In—Action/Conflict—Out.**

By thinking in scenes, you are focusing on the nitty-gritty of the emotional drama that is pulling along your story's plot, infusing it, through the depiction of conflict and character development, with emotional power.

When you start out with your book idea, you need to develop a growing awareness of your characters' feelings and needs. The scene translates the emotional life of those characters into visually powerful, engaging, and dramatic material—in other words, into scenes that work the same way in your book as they would in a film.

In the movie *The Fugitive*, for example, the inexperienced writer would think that the important powerful scenes in the movie are the murder of Dr. Richard Kimble's wife at the beginning, Dr. Kimble's fight with the one-armed man, and then the subsequent train crash that provides Kimble's escape and propels the movie into the major conflict of the story, the clash of goals between Kimble and U.S. Marshal Gerard, who is determined to recapture him.

While these scenes are important, actually, the most pivotal scene structurally, at the start of the film, is the confrontation in the culvert above the waterfall, where Kimble shouts at Gerard in pleading desperation, "I didn't kill my wife!" and the marshal says, "I don't care!" That scene not only works on a powerful emotional level, it also redefines the goals for the characters for the rest of the movie.

## HARRY'S TALE: GOALS AND STRUCTURE

Here's another example: Say you're working on your book, and you reach a section where you think, *Harry needs money. He's in debt*. How best do you dramatize that piece of plot information?

You don't have him come right out and say, "I'm broke, I need money." That's emotionally weak, and plotwise it's boring. What would *you* do in Harry's situation? Who would you go to for $10?

Well, $10 isn't a dramatic sum to begin with. The stakes for the action in the story aren't high enough to really engage us emotionally. But what if Harry needs $500,000, instead? And if he doesn't come up with it the kidnappers will kill his daughter or his wife will die because she won't be able to pay for the medical treatment she so desperately needs.

Try to envision the scene in which Harry goes to the bank to get a loan. If that doesn't work, you can envision the scene in which Harry goes to the bank with a gun to commit a robbery. You can also have a scene where perhaps Harry goes to his cousin Arnold to beg and borrow money. Maybe Harry goes to the racetrack and plunks down two hundred bucks on a horse in the eighth race.

All of those are scenes that show Harry's need for money.

With all these options, you need some guiding principle to choose which is the best dramatization to go with. That is often dictated by what you decide the book is going to be about thematically, what is the most emotionally powerful choice, who this character is and how far he will go to achieve his goal, in this case getting $500,000. What is Harry's state of mind?

## JUST WHAT IS A SCENE, ANYWAY?

Before starting to write your scene, ask yourself two questions:

- Does this scene advance the story in some way?
- What is this scene about?

Although it's not obvious, these questions are almost synonymous.

Within the scene, the dynamic should always be the same. So when you ask yourself what the scene is about, your answer should almost always take into account your main character. Does the scene move the readers closer to learning something important about that character? Do the dramatized events ultimately move her toward her long-term goal or prize? Your character should encounter opposition and obstacles that create conflict, and often moral or ethical dilemmas the character must resolve in order to move forward.

Having roughly figured that out, you can start to frame the scene.

A scene occurs at a set time and place. If events don't happen at a specific time and in a definite place, you're not writing a scene, you're writing an abstract narrative.

Here are some examples of scenes:

- a week from today in the dentist's office
- the first of March in a casino
- Thursday afternoon in a florist's shop

Each of the above examples contains the basic building blocks of a scene: They all contain a definite and recognizable place and a time.

Let's take Harry's story and develop it.

It is Thursday afternoon in a florist's shop near the hospital. Harry is buying flowers on his way to the hospital to visit his wife, Julie, who is undergoing another series of difficult medical treatments. She is very sick. What we don't yet know is that Harry has lost his job, his medical insurance has run out and he desperately needs $500,000 to pay Julie's medical treatment.

If you cross the "timeline" and go, say from Thursday afternoon to Friday morning, you've left the scene. If you cross the "placeline," it might be the same day but you're no longer in the flower shop; instead you're down at the corner church or at the hospital reception desk. Again, you've changed the scene. Whenever you change the time or the place of a scene, you create another scene.

## Leave Nothing to Chance

So you can envision the basic structure of your scene this way: Here's a character, here's his prize, and here's what's trying to stop him from achieving that prize.

If nothing is getting in your character's way, the scene won't work. If your character doesn't want something badly enough, again, the scene won't work because there will be no emotional power driving it. The reader has no real reason to be interested in the outcome of the scene (or, ultimately, the story) because the character doesn't really care enough about what is happening. There's a direct relationship between a character's emotional need to achieve a particular goal and the reader's active interest and involvement in the narrative. If the character doesn't care what's going to happen in the narrative, neither will the reader.

Everyone and everything is in the scene for a reason, and everyone in the scene has his own agenda. There's a good reason why Harry is in the florist shop on Thursday afternoon: He always buys flowers for his wife when he visits her in the hospital. But *this time*, the time that appears in your story, it's because of something more important than that. He has to somehow tell her that the bank is going to foreclose on their house tomorrow and the bailiffs are going to throw them out into the street because they are destitute.

## GEORGE'S STORY: THE IMPORTANCE OF CONFLICT

George's ultimate goal in your novel is to be the head of a big corporation (such as Microsoft or Exxon). Within the scene you're writing, George's immediate goal is to get a promotion and a raise.

If you write the scene so that George goes into his boss's office and says, "I want a promotion," and his boss says, "Hey, that's great, George, here you go. Here's your promotion, and while you're at it, here's a raise, too," you don't have much conflict or drama and you have absolutely no emotional content. In fact, there's no scene.

What if, instead, George goes into his boss's office and the boss says, "I absolutely cannot give you a promotion." George says, "Oh, I'm sorry I bothered you," and leaves. Again, no conflict, no scene.

But if George's boss says, "We can't give you a promotion, and before you ask, we don't have enough money to give you a raise," and George says, "Well, that may be true, but what we do have is a result of all the work I did last year. I deserve a promotion," and the boss says, "Well, your work wasn't *that* good," and George says, "What are you talking about? I won all kinds of awards . . ."

*Now*, you have conflict. The characters are going back and forth, and you have a scene because George is trying to attain a goal, in this case a promotion and a raise, and someone is trying to stop him.

What has to happen in the scene is that either George achieves his immediate goal against all odds or he doesn't. The important thing, though, is that when the scene is over, George has changed his relationship to his overall goal. There's been some sort of movement in the story development. It might be forward movement or it might be backward movement, but it's not static. If George leaves that office in exactly the same place he came in, in effect nothing has happened, so don't bother to write the scene. Don't fool yourself into thinking that if nothing *plotwise* happens in a scene, but it nevertheless shows *character development*, that's enough. It isn't. Scenes need to show *both* character development *and* plot development to be effective.

On a larger scale, the "promotion scene" fits structurally into George's overall goal this way: He either gets his promotion or he doesn't. If he gets his promotion, that's obviously a step up in the corporation. So he's closer to reaching his goal. If he doesn't get his promotion, he's been humiliated, he's been told he's not good enough, he might even quit the job. It's hard to become the head of a company if you quit it halfway through your first year there. But perhaps this setback is just what George needs to finally galvanize him into taking the kind of ruthless actions necessary to become the CEO of the company. Whatever the outcome of the scene, George has changed his relationship to the ultimate goal by the end of the scene. That's the important thing.

## THE FOUR MAIN ELEMENTS OF A GOOD SCENE

**1. Cause and effect relationships exist all the way along.** Each scene should cause a subsequent scene to occur.

**2. A scene has a goal.** An example is the scene in which

George wants a promotion. The scene is important and relevant because it's driven by the character's needs and wants.
He's trying to get something; there's a reason he came to that
room on that particular day.

**3. Each main character in a scene has a strategy.** That
strategy is what the character says and does, in terms of drama-
tizable actions, in order to get what he wants. Within that
scene, a character may try a number of strategies to get what
he wants before he succeeds—or fails.

**4. The ending of the scene must move us forward in
some way.** The movement of the scene is important; the character must have changed his position, relative to the end of
the story, for the scene to be worthwhile.

Even though a scene has its own plot list, its own inciting
incident, its own goal, and its own strategy, it's important to
remember that each scene links to the next.

Let's look at the *inciting incident*. What has caused the
events in the scene? If you've been sending your manuscripts
out, perhaps an editor or agent has commented that your work
is episodic. What that means is that the inciting incident in
your scene is occurring too often within each scene without
real regard for the scenes that have happened before or will
happen next.

Ideally, when you write a scene, the inciting incident—that
is, the thing that propelled your character into the florist's
shop on a Thursday afternoon, for example—happened in a
previous scene. It can be one scene ago, perhaps it was several
scenes before. (What we're touching on here is the importance of foreshadowing, which we'll look at in more detail in
chapter eleven on pacing. It's enough to know here, however,
that foreshadowing is not just a way of familiarizing a reader
with what is to come, but it acts as a spur to future action in
the story.)

If you go through your manuscript and analyze the scenes
in it, you may notice that the inciting incident for a scene

occurs *within* the scene rather than before it. If so, this inciting incident is also independent of other scenes and is not really linked, in any material or emotionally charged way, with any other scene in the story. In effect, at best you've written a series of barely related short stories.

## SARA AND ALISON, PART 1: EPISODIC AND NONEPISODIC NARRATIVES

This story illustrates the problem of unrelated, or independent, scenes. Although this is fiction, it could just as easily be nonfiction, as episodic writing is one of the primary problems for the unwary and inexperienced narrative nonfiction writer:

Sara, a mother, and her daughter Alison learn that Rick, the divorced father who lives in California, has died, leaving them a house. So the women decide to drive from New Jersey to California in order to sell Rick's house and use the money to fix up their own house back on the East Coast.

They get in the car and get just past Philadelphia when they find themselves in a snowstorm—a major snowstorm with ten-foot drifts and high winds, the kind of storm where people walk six feet outside their front doors and get lost because visibility is next to zero. Well, amazingly they survive that storm and get to Chicago where they pick up a female hitchhiker. Next thing they know, the hitchhiker pulls out a gun and robs them of just about everything they have. Luckily, most of their money was in traveler's checks, so after reporting what happened to the police, they get American Express to reimburse them. The police recover the women's car, which has been abandoned after it ran out of gas, and return it.

The two women go on. They reach Denver. In the diner they stop at for a meal, Alison falls in love with the short-order cook, who is a real good-looking guy, and she has a romance that lasts about a week. Lo and behold, he turns out to be a scoundrel, and he takes off with all her money. She's heartbroken, but mother and daughter go on. Finally they get to California, they get to the house and they manage to sell it.

This story is episodic, and the reason it's episodic is that there's no linkage between one event and the next. Any one of these incidents could have happened without the others happening. They all have their own *internal* inciting incidents. They are separate; they are not cause and effect.

If you write this way, all you do is write a bunch of stuff that happens haphazardly to some people. It is not a story, and an editor or an agent may well say to you, "You write well, but structurally your story is off."

This is one of the major problems of writing narrative nonfiction. How do you take a bunch of incidents that might all be true and part of the story you've been told or researched and turn them into a coherent story? What you need to do is find some way of pinning all the incidents together.

In fiction, you might do it as shown in the second part of Sara and Alison's story. In nonfiction, you would pore through the story searching for some inciting incident that has echoes throughout the rest of the story.

## SARA AND ALISON, PART 2: CAUSE AND EFFECT

Let's say that during the snowstorm in Philadelphia, Sara and Alison pick up a hitchhiker who turns out to be a runaway prostitute. Her pimp is chasing her, and if he catches up to her, he will kill the hooker and the mother and daughter as well.

Well, in Chicago he catches up with the three women and hijacks their car, forcing them to drive to a remote area. However, through a combination of daring, intelligence, and courage the women manage to overpower him long enough to escape.

When they get to Denver, though, the three women are pulled over by the cops and arrested, because the pimp has made a complaint to the cops, saying the women robbed him and stole his car. Well, finally they get out of that situation and manage to continue their journey to California.

That is a story. Why? Because even though it's terribly melodramatic and clichéd, everything that happens to these women is related to the fact that they picked up this hitch-hiker. That key scene is the inciting incident for most of the story that follows.

## THE SCENE THAT ISN'T

Let's look at an example of what can happen when you write a scene that really isn't a scene. You've written something that's kind of moody, and you think it's rather pretty, but it doesn't contain the four main elements of a good scene.

Suppose a young girl named Melanie is wandering through a field, picking flowers and just feeling happy. She's dreamy and observing the world around her in glorious detail: The reds are a wonderfully deep vermilion, the oranges a glowing sun color, the grass a rich green, the air thick with floating blossoms and the heady scent of a myriad of flowers, and so forth. Melanie is thinking about romance, but not with any particular person, just "Wouldn't it be nice . . ." thoughts, and you end up writing something pretty, but not exciting. You say to yourself, How can I save this section? It's the best thing I've ever written. How can I make it into a scene?

The answer is to go back and look at the items on your plot list and see how each applies.

What's the goal in the scene? What's Melanie's prize? Per-haps, under all this joy and light, Melanie is an abused child. She wants her mother's love, somebody's love, so she's pick-ing flowers in the hopes they'll please her mother. (Already, we've added the element of conflict and darkness, you may notice. Now the scene has a shape and direction. The scene— and the story—will take a variety of different directions and outcomes depending on who we decide Melanie really is. Characters in conflict lead to plot development.)

What's the inciting incident? Perhaps before this scene mother and daughter had yet another fight.

What's the strategy? What's the movement? Melanie is going to deliver those flowers, and one of two things is going to happen: Her mother's going to be very touched or . . . You figure it out for yourself.

Whatever the result is, you can look at the scene you've written, go through the plot list and make up things that fit and you'll have a scene.

## LINKING SCENES

If a scene introduces important new information, it should be dramatized as *direct narrative*.

Passages of time or events of secondary importance to the story's movement can be written as narrative bridges or transitional passages (*indirect narrative*), in the same way that dialogue can be written as direct or indirect speech.

Let's assume, in the following example, we have a lot of new and important information the reader hasn't seen before. The scene is written in a dramatized or direct narrative form.

### Direct Narrative

Harry examined the carnations. As he reached toward a bunch of mixed pink and red, he noted, almost with detachment, that his hand was shaking. The events of the last week or so were so overwhelming he could feel nothing yet—a numbness possessed him like an anesthetic he dreaded wearing off. It was all falling apart, like petals from one of the blooms in front of him. His right hand brushed past a bunch of flowers as he stretched toward those at the back, and a pink petal floated to the floor—there went his job; another petal peeled away—there went his home. Even as he examined the delicate stems of the flowers looking for imperfections, weeding out those with blooms past their prime, petals continued to drop away—his bank account, his car, his home . . .

At the cash register, Harry reached for his credit card to pay for the flowers—carnations were Julie's favorites and he always took them to her, carefully arranging them with some spindly looking green ferns in a vase he had brought from home and placed beside her bed—

then realized he no longer had it. The waiter in the restaurant last week, with what Harry considered a malevolent flourish, had cut it up in front of him and his guest. Harry pulled several crumpled bills from his pocket and smoothed them out, intently examining each for the correct change while the store owner waited patiently.

What have you learned? Harry is in trouble, he's stressed out, his wife is in need of cheering up, and so forth.

## Indirect Narrative

If this same passage is written as a link or bridging section between two scenes, however, we can assume all of the above information has already been conveyed to the reader. So we can make the passage much shorter and less cinematic. All we are really trying to accomplish in the example below is to get the characters from scene A, Harry buying flowers, to scene B, Harry's visit with his wife in the hospital. We might be able to simply write it this way:

That afternoon, Harry bought a bunch of carnations and busied himself arranging them in a vase as he waited for her to wake up.

It's pretty basic, but it does the job, and it may well be all we need in the circumstances.

## Transitions of Time

A commonly used bridging technique between scenes is simply to leave a white space between one scene and the next. It's the equivalent of a jump cut in a movie.

Sometimes scenes that could be separated by a white space could be linked by a simple, brief bridging passage so the narrative prose flows better.

For example, if a reader needs to be told how much time has passed between scene A and scene B, we can add a bridging link:

> Two days later, George again found himself in his boss's office preparing to fight for his promotion,

or,

> It had been two weeks since Harry had last heard from the bank . . .

The deftness with which you construct the narrative *journey* you're going to take the reader on, through foreshadowing, character motivation, and the artistic striptease of revealing just the *right* amount of narrative detail, takes real skill.

It's really only the second or third time we read a well-crafted piece, when we know where we are going, that we can really appreciate the technical excellence of how the writer got us there.

The key to layering a scene, that is, having more than one thing happening, is to give the reader a sense of the story before the story becomes more and more complicated. Eventually, these complications will be resolved. In the case of narrative nonfiction, an episodic construction can be seen as a narrative that brings in new information and new time frames without warning, only to make the same points already made in the story.

## EXERCISES

1. Consider the following situation: A woman is trying to get a set of keys from her husband.

Now, examine it for an inciting incident, a goal or prize, a strategy, and a resolution.

Before you start to write the exercise above, ask yourself: Is this taking place in a definite place? At a specific time? Is it a good scene, and if not, what's wrong? If there's no conflict, it's not good drama, and therefore it's not a good scene. With opposition, you have a story, because a story is about characters overcoming obstacles and opposition.

2. Here's another example to use to repeat the previous exercise: A man has to baby-sit a headstrong five-year-old.

3. Train yourself to ask questions of your plot and your characters: Who is he? What does he want? Why is he there? What is the child's problem? Now try writing the scene.

4. Some advice worth considering: The actor Christopher Walken says that when he considers how best to act a role, he first "works out" all the obvious stuff about his character, and then "flips it" doing something else, something unexpected.

With this advice in mind, completely rewrite the above scenes from memory.

# Chapter Eight

# Systems and the Status Quo

Imagine a row of dominoes standing next to each other. If you hit the first domino, it will strike the next domino, and that in turn strikes a third and so on, until a chain reaction has taken hold. Cause and effect relationships exist all the way to the end.

Similarly, your story is not just a series of events that have something in common, such as they all occurred on Monday or they all happened to a man named Marvin; they are events that are interrelated. A affects B, which affects C and so on.

Remember we talked about two basic story types: Someone goes on a journey, and someone knocks on the door.

If you think about these two story types, it's easy to see that both need the stimulation of an inciting incident to upset the existing system, or status quo, and launch the story.

## STATUS QUO

The *status quo* exists when everything is humming along without conflict and everyone is more or less content. It is when a system is functioning normally, in other words, the state of affairs at the start of your story.

Suppose you have a father, mother, son, and daughter. They're all connected. They are a family—a system. They are also a story system because they are main actors in your book and what one does affects the lives of the others. At first everything is going along fine. As in a well-tuned electrical system, the current is flowing nicely and there are no problems. You have a status quo.

But, when you introduce an inciting incident, something new enters the system and changes and upsets this status quo.

What if the inciting incident in your story is the "other man." He comes into the family system, meets the mother, and they start an affair.

This affair is naturally going to create a lot of conflict between the father and the mother.

Now the son is concerned. The father wants a divorce and the son thinks Dad's overreacting, that if they all pull together they can somehow get past this problem. The son feels that if only the father waits until the affair blows over, everything will return to the way it was. "Don't be rash, Dad, don't act hastily," he urges. So now the son is in conflict with the father.

The daughter, on the other hand, is mad at the mother for having the affair. "How could you do this to us?" she screams at her. Meanwhile, the son and the daughter disagree about what is going on and what should be done about it, and they're at odds, as well.

In frustration, the daughter starts acting out. She drinks, stays out all night, smokes pot, hangs out with a rough crowd. She dates a Hell's Angels biker who lives in a trailer park in the rough part of town. The daughter's behavior is distressing to the mother, and soon she and the daughter are fighting all the time. In short, everybody's mad at everyone else. There's a lot of excitement, a lot of passion, a lot of confusion—everything in the family system is out of whack. But, in the course of the story, they work through their problems and their crises and their conflict. At some point, ideally the climax or conclusion of your story, this element intruding into the family system is removed like a splinter or piece of grit. The "other man" tells the mother, "I can't deal with all this pressure and madness. I love you, but I can't be with you anymore," and he gets in his car, and he leaves.

## CONFLICT

So, what happens? In time, all the family members get back their equilibrium, they calm down and the status quo is re-established. The system is restored to balance.

The Hell's Angel tires of the daughter and takes off, the daughter and the mother make up, the son and the father come to an understanding and, now that the parents have kissed and made up, the daughter and the son become friends again. The family system comes back into balance. But . . .

All of the characters have been affected by what happened. They are no longer exactly the same. They have been changed by what happened in the story. So the old saying is true: As much as you would like to, you can't go home again. It is a law of nature that things are in a constant state of change, evolution, and decay. This is true of all systems, and your stories should reflect this, because your stories are systems like any other.

What happened in the example? Something came in and knocked the family system around. Like the group of dominoes standing in a line, one falls, they all fall.

An interesting exercise in seeing how this all works is to compare the movies *Return of the Secaucus Seven*, by John Sayles, and Lawrence Kasdan's *The Big Chill*. The parallels between the two movies are remarkable, although Sayles's movie was made first on a much lower budget. In Sayles's movie, the characters get together for a long weekend to relive old times and renew old friendships. Sayles's movie has a sly, almost satirical edge to it as the friends find themselves forced to confront the authorities (as they did while involved in 1960s campus activism) as the result of a ludicrous situation over a dead deer.

What is fascinating about the structure of these films when they are compared, however, is that in Kasdan's film, also about a group of old friends who get together for a long weekend, one of the characters has been removed from the system. In this movie, the characters are drawn together to mourn the death of one of their friends. The tone is much darker, and the influence of the past is much more about the experiences of the individual members than about their collective experience as a group.

## Ordinary People

Similarly structured, but more effective in my opinion, is Judith Guest's novel *Ordinary People*. Here, once again, an element has been removed from the family system.

Before the story begins, there were two sons, a mother, and a father. However, at the onset of the story, the family system has changed. One of the sons has drowned. In effect, he has been pulled out of the system. And his absence is as noticeable and as powerful an inciting force as the addition of the "other man" was in the earlier example.

The important thing is not simply that the drowning affects each person in the system, but that it also causes them to affect one another; it reverberates throughout the system in a great example of cause and effect.

As you begin to think about your story, you want to include elements that are not just thrown in there willy-nilly, but that play into the system, that influence everything.

## THE BACKSTORY

Let's work through an example.

Suppose a man who is unemployed and broke meets an attractive woman who is rich. He decides he is going to take advantage of this woman, pull some sort of a confidence scam, and cheat her out of her money.

The problem is he falls in love with her. That's the conflict.

Your first question should be, What's the backstory? How did this guy end up broke and unemployed in the first place? And what is it about him that allows him to go from being a crook and a cheat to a lovable character?

Your backstory should not be just a set of circumstances to explain a situation. It is really a *story* that took place before your main story's action begins. More likely, your backstory is made up of the high points of this story recalled briefly in flashback, and at the least, it's a single traumatic event in a character's life that influences the main story. In the case of your con man, what might be his backstory?

Well, what if this guy, Frank, had a vicious divorce. His wife, Eileen, took all his money and the house. Not content with that, she started calling his boss and saying terrible things about him to get him fired. Frank is really angry with women. He's decided he's going to get even with all women by picking on one, and then by cheating and lying to her. The problem, of course, is that he falls in love with his victim.

## The Oyster and the Pearl

By playing the appropriate elements of the backstory against the main story, you can see how one "irritates" the status quo into a dynamic system, in other words, a story filled with incident and conflict. This is a little like introducing a piece of grit inside an oyster shell, which in turn forces the oyster to produce a pearl. The introduction of the backstory (grit) into the system (oyster shell) produces an irritation or conflict that creates the main story (pearl).

To see a comic version of this particular type of story, rent the movie *Dirty Rotten Scoundrels*, starring Michael Caine and Steve Martin. (It's actually a remake of an earlier film, *Bedtime Story*, with Marlon Brando and David Niven, which is also worth watching.)

## The Goodbye Girl

Let's talk about your backstory for a moment and how it plays into the story system.

Do you recall Neil Simon's movie/play *The Goodbye Girl*?

First, let's set up the system. Paula (Marsha Mason) has an apartment in New York City with a spare room, and she is rolling along nicely, having finally adjusted to her boyfriend leaving her. What is going to upset this system? The arrival of a new element, or change, in that system.

In this case, the new element is Richard Dreyfuss's character, Elliot, an ambitious young actor in town to play Richard

III in an outrageous off-off-off Broadway production of the Shakespeare play. Paula's old boyfriend, as a parting gesture, has given Elliot a front door key, taken money from him, and told him the apartment—Paula's apartment—is all his.

Well, in the backstory, Mason's character has fallen in love three or four times with actors, and they always treated her poorly, then abandoned her.

What's going to happen to her in the present-time story? Is she going to fall in love with a pig farmer? Of course not. She's going to fall in love with another actor. Why? Because the best drama and conflict arise from forcing a character to experience and deal with the very thing she doesn't want to cope with, in this case, falling in love with yet another actor. By forcing your central character to confront her inner and outer demons, you are ratcheting up the emotional power of the narrative and consequently the reader's involvement with the unfolding story.

## HOW AND WHY

Writers are often told to "start a story with a bang," and some authors think that instruction should be obeyed literally. However, the purpose of beginning a story with a dramatic moment is to engage the readers' emotions from the opening paragraph and then hold their interest by posing a problem or a dilemma of an extreme moral or ethical nature. How did this character reach this traumatic point in her life? And how will she solve this problem? It is the readers' emotional commitment to what the main character is going through and their intellectual fascination with how that character will solve her problems that will compel the readers to keep turning the page.

The *depth* or severity of the conflict a character has to cope with will provide a parallel emotional depth for your story system.

The *change* of the status quo system into a dynamic, evolving system will give you the story's problem and, ultimately, its solution, in other words, the plot. This change, or plot development, comes from asking of your story and its characters the question why?

Examine another story. This one may sound familiar.

A successful businessman is visited by three ghosts. The three ghosts say to him, "In order for you to be happy, you had better be a nice guy, you'd better be generous, and you'd better be thoughtful."

The status quo system then is an unhappy man, with no friends and a lot of enemies.

So in the backstory is this a guy a nice person? Or, more to the point, what happened to him in the backstory to turn him into this sour miser?

Of course, we're talking about Scrooge in Charles Dickens's *A Christmas Carol*. Scrooge, you may recall, was stingy and pretty nasty.

In the main story, he's being asked to run against his nature. But that nature was formed by an unhappy love affair when he was a young man that forever changed his nature—at least until the time the story starts. Scrooge's backstory is affecting the system of the main story by asking him to rebel against the kind of man he's made himself into and overcome that traumatic event of his youth to recapture the fun-loving guy he used to be.

## EXERCISES

For each of the following situations, come up with a back-story, that is, something about the character's past that is going to affect the way he behaves in the present and will intrude upon and change his system.

1. A father desperately wants to help his teenage son who has been accused of a serious crime, but the father is unable to bring himself to do anything.

What is it in his past that is affecting that family/story system?

2. A young woman is planning to commit a murder in order to win a writing fellowship. What is it that happened in the past that makes this scholarship so important?

# Chapter Nine

# Conflict

I want to introduce you to Ted and Patty. They first appeared in an article in *Writer's Digest* magazine that Gary wrote called "Just Say No":

> Hard-working Ted had a crush on Patty. One night at the Moose Lodge, though limping slightly from a hockey injury, Ted asked Patty to dance, and she said, "Yes." Then, he asked her if she'd like to go bowling sometime, and she said, "Yes, that would be splendid, Ted." Well, Ted got more and more infatuated with Patty and so he asked her to go steady. Patty said, "Yes." Before long Ted and Patty were in love, and on a drizzly Tuesday afternoon at the coin laundry, Ted got down on his knees and asked Patty to marry him. Patty said, "Yes." Ted said he wanted to live in Elgin, Illinois, and Patty said, "Yes, I would love that, Ted, more than anything, more than chocolate covered cherries, and I want us to have three babies, okay?" Ted said, "Yes." So they moved to Elgin, where Ted applied for a job at the rope factory, and they had three healthy kids and lived happily ever after.

Not exactly the stuff of cliff-hanging suspense—or any kind of suspense, come to that. In fact, it's a pretty lousy story.

Now, in real life when people say yes to us or people we like, we always feel great, but in good storytelling, saying yes the way it happens in Gary's Ted and Patty story is not so great. In fact, it's terrible. Done this way, it's the worst of all crimes a writer can commit; it's boring. Readers rarely get more than a page or so into a story like this before their eyes glaze over and they put it aside to watch the more interesting nationally televised darts championship or turtles racing.

## THE BASIS OF ALL NARRATIVE

Narrative storytelling is all about conflict. Between us, Gary and I have written a lot of stuff that's been published. But we have a lot more pieces sitting in trunks that will never get published, at least in their current form. There are probably a lot of reasons for that, principally that they're not very good. But if there's a single reason why these books will remain unpublished, it's because they lack conflict.

Conflict is the basis of drama, whether it's fiction or re-created narrative nonfiction. If you don't have a series of scenes with some sort of conflict in them, you don't have a narrative.

As I mentioned earlier, Sigmund Freud, despite criticisms that have been leveled at him in recent years, offers a range of provocative ideas about dreams, childhood, love, authority and many other things, all of which comprise the matter of conflict in narrative storytelling. Perhaps one of the most useful concepts he came up with was the psyche. This can be broadly defined as that part of ourselves that is responsible for our individual thoughts and feelings—the seat of the faculty of reason.

What Freud maintained, and should be of some interest to the student of narrative storytelling, is that despite our outward appearances and despite our wishes to the contrary, we are not unified beings. Emphasized and highlighted by the "political correctness" movement, which at its best underscores sensitivity to the nuances of others and at its worst tries to homogenize society, there is a great movement these days to make art "nice." No controversy, no conflict. According to Freud, character *is* conflict. When we dream, the top slides off the cauldron of our emotions and we see another self, far less shackled by convention and the niceness of civilized behavior than when awake. At night, we discover that nothing is foreign to us: Murder, cruelty, sexual urges of all sorts arise directly or in distorted forms within the dreaming theatre of our minds. And they arise, Freud says, because they are reflections of our desires. At night, we discover what our dark persona is and what it wants. And from this yarn, we weave the warp and weft of the whole cloth that will eventually comprise narratives about ourselves and our world.

Drama is about the resolution of a character's problems and dilemmas. And problems and dilemmas arise when someone says, "You can't do that" or, "You mustn't do this." In short, conflict is about someone saying no.

A narrative can be thought of as a series of connected conflicts (with bridging passages in between) that are eventually resolved by one final, cathartic conflict.

When there's no conflict on the page, there's no reader interest in what happens. The reader also has no emotional involvement in the story. In other words, the audience doesn't much care what your characters do, why they're doing it, or what happens to them. Nothing is compelling the reader to stay with that story. Conversely, the more extreme the conflict, the more emotionally involved in your narrative your reader becomes. One way to do this is to make sure your characters have individual goals that will clash and conflict. Drama is about the fight for dominance among a group of characters.

## THREE TYPES OF CONFLICT

We can divide conflict into three basic types.

### Man Against Man

This is the most common conflict. In a scene, two people— men, women, or children, in any combination—may not necessarily be having a fight, but there's something antagonistic between them. Great examples of this are the movie *The Fugitive* and Elmore Leonard's novel *Get Shorty*, and I'm sure you can think of many more. In *The Fugitive*, the conflict comes from the clash of goals between U.S. Marshal Gerard, who is single-minded in his pursuit of escaped prisoner Richard Kimble, and Kimble's need to (1) find the one-armed man who really committed the murder and then (2) get Gerard to help him arrest the masterminds who ordered the murder in the first place. In *Get Shorty*, everyone has clashing goals and ulterior motives, but they circle around an "unreachable" stolen bag of money, stashed away in a locker at Los Angeles International Airport, and the desire of criminals and low lifes to achieve mainstream legitimacy through the wealth and fame that making a hit movie will bestow on them.

## Man Against Nature

You may have a guy trying to climb a mountain and there's a hurricane coming into town, or a tornado, flood, whatever. A famous example of man against nature is *Moby Dick*. In Melville's classic, a whaling captain is obsessed with hunting down and killing the only beast that ever bested him at sea, a beast that not only escaped but took away the captain's leg in the process. Another example is Hemingway's *The Old Man and the Sea*, which is a reworking of the themes of *Moby Dick*, in this case, an old fisherman's obsession with catching a big fish before he dies.

## Man Against Himself

This involves internal conflict and is the hardest to write well. The danger is that the writer's fascination with the character is not translated onto the page or conveyed well to the reader and the story becomes static, wordy, self-involved, and boring. The trick here, so to speak, is to find ways of dramatizing in an external fashion what is going on in the internal story. Edgar Allan Poe's "The Tell-Tale Heart" or Dostoyevsky's *Crime and Punishment* are about criminals who are left with the gnawing, mounting guilt that murder can inflict on a normal human being, and the major concern of both stories is how the characters wrestle with this guilty conscience. Daniel Defoe's

*Robinson Crusoe*, about a man who is shipwrecked on a desert island and forced to survive alone for years before he is rescued, is another example.

One source of this kind of internal conflict is regret. Another, as we've mentioned, is the guilt of people who don't have the strength to do what they have to do, such as quit drinking, stop taking drugs, etc. In general, this type of story works best in a short form rather than a long form.

## EQUAL BUT OPPOSITE

Conflict should be two forces in opposition, but they should be at least somewhat equal when seen from the point of view of the main character. In fact, the hero of a story is pretty much defined by the strength of the opposition she has to overcome. Strong opposition also increases the emotional potency of the narrative because the greater the conflict, the higher the stakes for all involved.

Imagine a football game: the New York Giants against Bristol Junior High School. Unless you are going to write a David and Goliath kind of story, it won't be a very interesting game, will it? The reason is that the conflict is not equal and thus the outcome is predictable. The Giants, one would imagine, would storm down the field and they would score, and then they would storm down the field and score again. There's not much Bristol Junior High could do that could stop them.

Seen from the perspective of someone on the Bristol team, however, you have a different kind of story with a high emotional content, one that isn't about winning, but about the intensity of the effort to win, the striving to be the best, to make your dreams a reality. The movies *Hoosiers* and *Hoop Dreams* both dealt wonderfully with this kind of story.

In your story, whatever is trying to stop your character from reaching her goal must be so formidable that all the way through the book readers wonder who's going to win the battle.

Stories are about characters trying to go in a specific direction and some force, some opposition, saying, ''No, you can't do that.''

One of the things Gary and I have noticed a lot in books by inexperienced writers is that as they write their books, they structure them so that at the beginnings of the narratives there are a couple of minor scenes, obviously building up to a big conflict—let's say there's going to be a big fight. But when readers get to that point, instead of the fight scene, they get, "The day after the fight, they went to . . ."

Don't be afraid of the big scene, the big fight, the big conflict, whatever it is. Think about the movie *Witness*. The cop, Harrison Ford, is forced to save the nonviolent Amish child from the clutches of desperate violent men determined to make sure the kid will not appear in court against them. Just how effective do you think this story would be without that final confrontation sequence in which viewers see and experience, in an almost cathartic way, the good guys being saved and the bad guys being vanquished?

Make sure your characters have goals that clash. The conflict is the best part of your book. That's what people read it for: to see those big scenes. It's the emotional payoff readers have been waiting for. To shortchange the readers is to leave them frustrated and annoyed. Almost certainly they will never read anything with your name attached to it again.

Some beginning writers, trying to echo their otherwise mature attitudes toward life, try to avoid conflict in narrative storytelling. Their characters act as the writers strive to act. In real life, confrontation can be very scary at least and dangerous at worse, so it makes sense if you're a bit afraid of it. But in narrative storytelling, you can't be afraid of conflict. It's the meat of drama.

## THE TEMPERATURE GAUGE

One way to think about conflict in your scene is to imagine your scene has a temperature. It has a low temperature (not much conflict), a high temperature (intense conflict) or some grade in between. In other words, temperature is a way of describing the intensity of the scene's emotional power. In general, you always want to maximize a story's emotional impact.

A low temperature means that Joe says to Harry, "Gee, Harry, I had a terrible day at work today," and Harry says, "No kidding? What happened?" There's no conflict here at all. Both Harry and Joe are going in the same direction.

Now, if Harry says, "I'm sick of all your whining and complaining. Don't you ever shut up?" he is clearly not interested in what Joe has to say, so you've raised the temperature a bit. There's a high degree of resistance, and the friction between these characters is clearly being established. Which version would you prefer to read more about?

You don't have to have a high temperature or a lot of conflict in every scene, but if you have several scenes in a row in which the temperature of the conflict is low, you're writing a dull book.

## HOW TO BUILD CONFLICT

You want to put pressure on a scene, and there are a couple of ways you can do that.

### Small Spaces

Conflict occurs because two different people with opposing goals are forced into a small space together. Imagine, for example, a log cabin in the mountains. A sudden winter storm forces two characters, Mr. Neatnick and Mr. Slob, to live together for a while. Neil Simon's play (and subsequent movie) *The Odd Couple* is exactly this kind of conflict and situation. The movie *The Defiant Ones*, with Tony Curtis and Sidney Poitier, actually shackled together a racist white convict with an aggressive black convict as they struggle to make good their escape from prison in the 1950s Deep South.

*The Defiant Ones*, directed by Stanley Kramer with an Academy Award-winning screenplay by Harold Jacob Smith and Nathan E. Douglas (blacklisted screenwriter and actor Nedrick Young) is a powerful movie that pulls few punches and was highly praised when it was released, appearing as it did in

1958 during a period of civil rights protests, sit-ins, and other political demonstrations in the black community. The New York Film Critics voted the movie Best Picture of the Year, and Stanley Kramer, Best Director. The symbolism, particularly the ending, may seem dated now, but it's a swift and exciting action film. It manages to entertain while at the same time dramatically explore its provocative symbolism. It provokes discussion that is still relevant to current problems of race relations, particularly in its metaphor of society captured in the memorable image of the two bound convicts, one black, one white, forced to deal with each other and the problems that beset them both in order to survive.

White convict Johnny "Joker" Jackson (Tony Curtis) and black convict Noah Cullen (Sidney Poitier) escape from a southern chain gang, fleeing from Sheriff Max Muller (Theodore Bikel) and his bloodhounds. The convicts must face tremendous difficulties, including the two-foot-long chain that shackles them together, hostile townspeople, a lynch mob, a swamp, and their own mutual hatred, belligerence, and bigotry. As they flee across the country, the two find they can't run from each other and must come to terms with their situation.

The white bigot and the sensitive but angrily resentful black man fight, argue, and pick at one another. Yet when they have to cross a river, the heavy current almost drowns Cullen until Jackson drags him to safety. "Thanks for pulling me out," Cullen says. "I didn't pull you out. I stopped you from pulling me in," says Jackson.

By the time they manage to free themselves of their physical shackles, a metaphorical bond has been forged between them, keeping them still bound together, highlighted by the final sequence at the railway tracks as the sheriff and his posse close in.

The two men pursue a freight train to escape. Cullen is able to jump onto one of the moving cars. He locks hands with his white companion (a memorable image of black and white hands and arms locked together), but he cannot pull Jackson up onto the moving train. So he sacrifices his own freedom and falls back off the train onto the ground.

In their final few moments of freedom, they share a cigarette, and Cullen sings the blues classic "Long Gone" as he cradles the weakened and injured Jackson while the sounds of the bloodhounds on their trail grow louder.

## The Ticking Clock

Another way of putting pressure on a scene is with a time limit. Consider a movie such as *48 Hrs*. What if someone said to the cop (Nick Nolte), "You can solve this crime and have this convict (Eddie Murphy) help you out, and you can keep him out of prison for several months if you like." Not very exciting. There's no pressure urging on the protagonists, nothing forcing them to act in a way that could get them into trouble and cause them to make mistakes because of haste and worry, thereby increasing the inherent drama and conflict of their situation.

But that's not how it happens. Someone says to the cop, "You've got forty-eight hours." This use of a time constraint as pressure is a typical device in a story. One of the classic examples is the movie *D.O.A.* (*Dead on Arrival*). Here, the hero, Edmond O'Brien, has been given a slow-acting poison. In a wonderful twist, the victim of a murder also becomes the detective and has twenty-four hours to find out who killed him and why.

Nobody ever says to a hero, "Take your time, you got ten years." Conflict is intensified by the pressure of time.

Here's a scene by Frank Strunk from *Jordon's Wager* (Walker). Strunk, who now has several well-received novels to his credit, was a student writer Gary and I helped to get published. This was Strunk's first novel. It's set in Appalachia in the 1930s.

Jordon is trying to solve the murder of a young girl called Bitsy Trotter. As is the case with any story like this, he needs to acquire information from a variety of people. That's his goal in many scenes: get information. In this particular scene, he's going off to see an old woman by the name of Rachel, and his goal is to get Rachel to give him some information that will help him solve the murder.

The important thing to understand here is that conflict doesn't mean necessarily that two people are in complete opposition. They may be total enemies, or they may be pretty much in agreement, but there should be some area of conflict, distrust, or disagreement between them that has to be overcome:

> The fat black cat with white front paws stopped washing its face and gave Jordon a heavy-lidded but thorough inspection. Then it turned to Rachel Blackwell and uttered a plaintive meow.
>
> "It's all right, darling," the old woman said, "he ain't staying." Looking at Jordon, she said, "Princess don't care for strangers. Specially menfolks." After a moment she added, "Can't say I do neither." Her voice was like the rustle of winter wind through a dead oak.
>
> She led Jordon toward some chairs in front of the smoldering fireplace. "Not there," she said, "that's mine. Here. Set over there."

As we analyze the building conflict in the scene we see that Rachel has thrown the first punch: "He ain't staying," she says, and adds, "Princess don't care for strangers. Specially menfolks. . . . Can't say I do neither."

Then she tells Jordan not to sit in *her* chair, being unwelcoming and territorial. The fight is on. However, Jordon is being restrained because he needs something from Rachel, and she's obviously resisting. What drives this scene now? We are forced to think about *why* she would resist and be instinctively hostile to Jordon. What is her involvement in all this? We like Jordon, so we are emotionally involved in seeing that he succeeds against these increasingly difficult odds—a desire to find the killer of a girl and an obstructive, obdurate old woman who seems to be an obstacle he must overcome along the way to reaching his goal of bringing a killer to justice.

What would happen if Jordon walked in and said, "I need some information," and Rachel said, "OK, here's the information"? There'd be no scene, no emotional involvement, no interest. If all the author was after was plot information he could do that, but narrative storytelling (fiction and nonfiction) is about the interaction of *characters* and their goals. It is the clash of these goals and the need to resolve the conflicts that arise from this clash—*not* just plot advancement—that make a story a page-turner.

So the conflict grows, the liquid in the cauldron bubbling more fiercely and gradually growing hotter as the temperature of the scene rises. Pay attention particularly to how Strunk develops the conflict in the scene and the choices he gives to his protagonist, Jordon:

> Rachel threw some slack coal from a bucket into her fireplace and stirred it with a poker. Flames from the rescued fire cast a flickering light on her ancient face. What could have been a smile played at the shriveled and shrunken lips which covered the three or four snaggled teeth she still had.
>
> Her hair was dyed a dull black, and the dark shapeless dress she wore hung loosely on her tiny body. Tiny, Jordon thought, like Bitsy Trotter. Rachel pulled a shawl around her bony shoulders and settled herself into her own chair, a cane-bottom rocker.
>
> "What is it you want?" she asked.
>
> "To talk about Bitsy Trotter," Jordon replied.
>
> "You've come to the wrong place."
>
> "I thought you might be able to help me. I'm trying to find out who killed her. You did know the girl, didn't you?"
>
> Rachel eyed him coldly for a moment before answering. "What makes you think I did?"
>
> "You don't live that far from the Trotters, through the woods. And I have information that you and Bitsy knew each other."

The cat arose from its throne across the room and made its way to Jordon, started rubbing against his shins. Why did cats always do that to him, he wondered. . . . Jordon was beginning to suspect that there was a secret network of some kind through which cats passed the message to one another: Berk Jordan hates to be rubbed against . . . make sure you do it. He didn't want to maybe rile the old woman up before he got started with her by pushing Princess away. So he let her rub. For the moment.

Rachel had not responded to his last comment, so he said,

"Did you know Bitsy Trotter?"

She stared at him with an expression he took to be distaste.

"I knowed her."

He's fighting to get information out of her, but she's still resisting, despite the fact that the cat has changed his mind about Jordon and that Jordon has decided to ignore his instinct to push the animal away:

"What can you tell me about her?"

"Nothing." She fixed her attention on the open fire.

"Can't or won't?"

"It's all the same, ain't it?"

"The law says different. In a court of law you'd have to tell."

Now we have it. Jordon has decided it's time for another tack. His first approach to this little battle had been, "Well, I'll be nice." But that hasn't worked, and so now he's resorted to, "The law says different." He's decided to use a threat, an indication that he has a stick and the determination to use it if he has to:

She looked at him and laughed. A dry cackle. "You believe that?" She studied him for a moment. "No sir," she said, "you don't look that dumb."

So much for the threat of a legal stick—or so it at first appears:

> "You don't care what the law says?" Jordon asked.
>
> "Do you?"
>
> "I do, yes."
>
> "Sure you do," she said in a voice heavy with sarcasm. "They's people out there right this minute fighting and stealing, gambling and whoring and selling whiskey. All against the law. And others, crooked as a barrel of fish hooks, swindling people out of their last scrip nickel." Her voice cut through the room's quietness, filled it with venom. "Others working men in little dog-hole mines till they're ready to drop over, then using fancy figuring to take back ever nickel they make just to keep a roof over their head and a little something in their families' bellies. You think all them people care about the law? You're supposed to be upholding it. Why ain't you out arresting some of them?"
>
> Not a bad question, Jordon had to admit. He said, "Right now I'm trying to catch the murderer of a young girl."
>
> "What they tell me, you're running for high sheriff, too," Rachel went on. "If you get elected, you going to arrest everybody that breaks the law?"
>
> Jordon parried. "You know me, then?"
>
> "Knowed you when you first stepped up on my porch. Know a lot more about you than you might think. Ain't a lot goes on in Stanton County I don't know about, mister."
>
> "But you won't talk to me about Bitsy Trotter. . . ."

What's happening here is that they are sparring, but despite herself, Rachel finds that Jordon is drawing information out of her, the temperature of the scene is beginning to cool, and they are slowly but surely starting to search for a middle ground—to do what in the East is called "save face."

Rachel says to him:

"You know folks say I'm a witch?"

"I've heard that.". . . .

"How about you?" Rachel asked. "You think I'm a witch?" . . .

Suddenly, she broke into a high, piercing laugh. Sitting there in her cane-bottom rocker, stroking her black cat, her head thrown back, shrieking laughter pouring from her, she looked the part. Jordon figured, by God, I might have spoke too soon. Maybe I should have said yes.

She stiffled her laughter long enough to say, "But I remind you of a witch, huh? Is that what you're thinking?"

At this, Jordon began to laugh. "Now that you mention it. . . ."

As they roared in laughter at themselves and each other, Princess jumped from Rachel's lap and went to the edge of the fireplace where she sat regarding them both with a look that might well have been contempt.

So now we've gone from no to yes. All that remains is for Jordon to give Rachel a reason to help him. Jordon says to her:

"Whatever you know about Bitsy might help me find out who killed her. But I reckon you'll have to be the judge of that."

They talk some more, and as Jordon is leaving Rachel says to him:

"They say you're a man who's got no love for the coal companies. . . . Is that so?"

"I reckon you could say that. I've never worked for them, except for three weeks once in the mines. Enough to convince me it wasn't for me."

And there it is! Their common ground, a mutual dislike of the mining companies, their practices, and how it enslaved the people of Appalachia. The conflict resolution begins. By the end of the scene, Rachel's thinking that maybe this Jordon guy ain't so bad, and maybe she will cooperate with him. As he leaves she says:

> "If I was to think of something that might help you,
> I'll let you know."

What's happened here is that first they had a conflict—Jordon trying to get Rachel to cooperate against her better judgment. She resisted, until toward the end, as they talked about the coal companies, Rachel discovered she and Jordon had something in common, and though not completely trusting him, she nonetheless agrees to give him some, if not all, of what he wants.

## JUST SAY NO

The idea of conflict can be reduced to the word *no*. Throughout a book, something or someone is saying no to your characters. Usually, it's a person or a number of people saying no. And they're saying no in the scenes and throughout the book. Each time someone says no to your protagonist it increases the narrative's emotional potency, depending on how you resolve the issue of overcoming that particular obstacle.

Let's examine *Compromising Positions*, a novel by Susan Isaacs. In this novel, about a woman who lives in the suburbs whose life is kind of dull, the protagonist becomes fascinated by the murder of a local dentist, who happened to be a bit of a ladies' man. The protagonist decides to snoop around and investigate this murder. What does her husband do? Does he say, "Oh, sure honey, that's a great idea"? Of course not. He says, "Don't do this. You're making a fool of yourself, you're embarrassing me, you're neglecting your duties at home."

What do the police say? "Oh, what a fine thing. You're going to help us get the murderer"? No. They say, "Stay out of it. Mind your own business."

No, no, no, no, no. That's what a narrative is, whether fiction or nonfiction: the conflict generated by people saying no to your characters and your main character in particular pursuing her goal anyway.

The problem is, within the scene, even though somebody or something is saying no to your character, you need to get the opposition to say yes by the end of the scene or you won't have much movement in your narrative. The question is, How are you going to get to this point?

## MAKE ME A BELIEVER

You can't just have characters say, "No. No, no, no, no. Oh, OK. Yes." It's going to seem contrived. Readers have to believe that something happened within that scene that got those characters to turn around and say yes.

In the *Jordon's Wager* excerpt, we saw Rachel go from no to yes because she and Jordon discover they have something in common—a mutual dislike of the coal companies.

You can get to yes a number of ways. You can get to yes by raising the payoff for something. For example, in a private detective's office, a beautiful woman comes in and says, "I want you to take my case. I want you to find my brother who's missing. He was last seen working on the docks in Boston."

The detective says, "No, I can't do that." The woman says, "Oh please."

"No."

They go back and forth until toward the end she says, "You know, I find you very attractive."

And he starts thinking, *Well, maybe I can do this.* He's gotten around to yes because she used seduction.

The reverse of that is some sort of coercive blackmail—a stick, as opposed to the carrot of seduction. A man in a black hat says to the detective, "I need you to take this mysterious box to California."

"What's in it?"

"I can't tell you."

"I'm not going to take it."

No, no, no. And finally, the man in the black hat says, "You know, I'd hate to see you have a bad accident—or maybe a friend of mine will give your daughter a ride home from school tomorrow." A threat. So our hero thinks, *When you put it that way. . . .* Readers understand how he got from no to yes.

But the most common way for getting from no to yes is something internal to the character. In this example, Jeff has been abandoned by his wife. He's kind of sad and goes off to be a big brother with a Big Brother/Big Sister organization. He's sitting at the table talking about this kid George, who may become his little brother. The counselor, who's telling Jeff about George, is not making young George sound too appealing. The counselor says, "Well, George is a nice enough kid, but he'll steal your stereo and who knows what else." Jeff thinks, *Maybe I don't want to work with this kid after all. No, I better not take him. No, no, no.*

But, as the interview goes along, the counselor says something about George not having a father, and Jeff says, "Let me ask you something. Was George abandoned?" The counselor says, "Yes, he was." And Jeff says, "OK, I'll work with him."

Why? Because Jeff's found out that he shares something in common with George: They've both been abandoned by people who at one time cared about them. Jeff now identifies with George, and readers can believe that emotional experience has gotten him from no to yes.

One more thing about conflict: Don't let it intensify too quickly. You don't want people coming into the room and spilling out all their conflict quickly with yelling and shouting. You want to play it a bit more subtly. Hold that lid on. Hold onto the conflict. Release it gradually.

## EXERCISES

1. Go through five scenes you've written and look for who or what is saying no and what she or it is saying no to. If you can't find a person, an event or a force saying no, you're going to have to rewrite the scene because there's no conflict.

2. Suppose a woman is dying of AIDS and her bitter, estranged husband can't forgive her for cheating on him and infecting their only child. How does she get him to forgive her as she lies on her death bed? Or does she? Write the scene.

# Chapter Ten

# Theme and Subplot

Whenever you mention to people that you're working on a book, they probably ask, "What's it about?" You may tell them, for example, "Well, it's about a woman who decides to buy a ranch in Arizona." But what if you had to give them a one-word answer?

The answer to that question is the *theme* of your book.

There should be in your narrative a single idea, echoed throughout the book at many levels. Maybe it's freedom. Maybe it's integrity, loyalty, regret, sorrow—something. This is the theme of your story.

In *Good If It Goes*, a young adult novel by Gary and his wife, Gail, the theme is tradition. It's about a Jewish boy who's soon to have his bar mitzvah but who would rather play basketball. And those things are in conflict. It's also about his relationship with his grandfather. But if it had to be reduced to a single word, the story is about tradition.

I'm going to show you a scene from Gary and Gail's book, and you'll see how this idea of tradition is woven into the narrative.

David is twelve years old. He's been informed that he's got to take Hebrew lessons on Tuesdays and Thursdays—the same days he wants to play basketball. He's not happy about it, and he talks to his mother and says I don't want to do this, and she says you've got to do this, you're Jewish, it's the tradition. He talks to his father, and his father says listen to your mother. So, he decides to go to his grandfather, Max Levene, and try to get his grandfather to convince his parents that he shouldn't have to go to Hebrew school, that he shouldn't have to bother with this tradition of the bar mitzvah.

The family goes to temple one morning, and after returning to the grandfather's house, Max says, "I take David for a walk." David is telling the story:

> Grampa led me down behind his house into some woods that stretch for about a mile, I guess, all the way to the turnpike. In the autumn here the leaves on the trees are gold and red and lots of other colors and on a sunny afternoon like this was, they're just incredibly bright. It was real basketball weather.
>
> "To the stream," Grampa said. There's a stream down behind Grampa's house, which is the main reason he bought the house years ago. He lived near a stream when he was a kid in Germany.
>
> "You know," Max Levene said as we moved down the hill kind of slowly because Max isn't all that young anymore, "when I was a boy in Germany my father would walk with me and my brothers and sisters down to the stream on the first day of Rosh Hashanah. There we would say a prayer and then we would shake out our pockets in the stream. It was said that we were shaking away our sins. This is a custom called *Tashlich*. Then we would walk home and Mama would be waiting with home-baked challa and wine and we would dip the challa in honey and everyone would wish everyone a sweet new year."
>
> When we got down by the stream, Grampa reached in his pockets and took out his handkerchief and his keys and put them on the ground by a tree. Then he stood by the stream and he yanked his pockets inside out and he shook them over the stream. "David," he said, "you got some sins you want to get rid of?"
>
> "I guess," I said, and I stood next to him and shook out my pockets, though I felt a little silly doing it.
>
> We sat for a while by the stream without talking and

then Max Levene said, "What is the problem?"

"Grampa," I said, "I've got to play basketball this year. This is absolutely my last chance. I'll never make the team next year in high school. I'm too short. Randy and I started the Shrimp League just so kids like us could play on a team."

"So why is this a problem?"

"Ma and Dad won't let me play," I said.

"Hmmn," Grampa said. He says "hmmn" a lot. "This is strange," he said. "Your mother and your father love you. Why would they not let you do something that is so important to you? They must have a very good reason."

"No, Grampa, they don't have any good reason."

"Oh? So what is this reason they have that is not so good?"

"Hebrew school."

"Hebrew school? This is a problem?"

"My bar mitzvah!" I said. "I'm getting my haftorah pretty soon and that means I have to go to Hebrew school twice a week to learn it. Tuesdays and Thursdays! And the Shrimp League games are on Tuesdays, and even if they weren't, there just wouldn't be time for everything, with homework and all."

"Hmmn," my grandfather said.

"It's just not fair, Grampa. I don't care about being bar mitzvahed. It's not important to anybody except them, but they won't listen to me. You're the only one who can convince them. They'll listen to you."

Grampa didn't say anything for a long time. He just stared at the stream. Then he said, "What makes you think that I would tell your parents you should not go to Hebrew school, my grandson?"

"Because you're an atheist," I said. "You don't believe in God."

"Agnostic," he said.

" 'Agnostic'? What's that?"

"It means I'm not sure about God."

"Well, if you're not so sure there's a God then you don't believe in bar mitzvahs, right?"

"My grandson," he said, "it is sometimes difficult for me to believe there is a God who should allow what has happened to my family and our people over the years. You know what I'm talking?"

"You mean about the Nazis and the concentration camps and all that?"

"Yes, David," he said. "All that." He said it more to himself than to me. Most of Max Levene's family had been killed in Germany because they were Jewish. "So," Grampa said, "this is not a God I can believe in, though I don't say you shouldn't. This you must decide for yourself. But I believe in our people, David, and it seems to me that if there is a God he would want you to be a bar mitzvah boy like your father before you. It is the tradition."

"I know, I know," I said. There was that word again. *Tradition.* "But Grampa," I said, "I don't believe in tradition."

"Oh?"

"Yeah, Grampa, really! I thought about it, I really did, and I think that what's going on now is what's really important, not a bunch of stuff that happened years ago."

"So you do not believe in tradition? Of this you are sure?"

"Yes," I said. "I'm sure."

"Oh," Grampa said, "I am so relieved. The money I will save."

"What are you talking about, the money you'll save?" I said. For a minute I thought Max Levene was getting nutty.

"On your birthday presents," he said. "And on Chanukah I'll save a fortune. Yes, yes. With all the money I'll save, I'll buy maybe a new car."

"Grampa, what have birthday presents got to do with it? And Chanukah presents?"

"It is tradition," he said. "Nothing more. Why do we give a present to a boy on his birthday? Because it is the tradition, that's why. And Chanukah. Tell me, David, your Christian friends, do they also think tradition is not important? Their parents will be happy to know this. No more Christmas shopping!"

"But that's different," I said. "Birthday presents and Christmas presents, that's not the same as being bar mitzvahed."

"I know," he said. "Being a bar mitzvah boy is even more important."

For a while we didn't say anything. . . .

Finally, Grampa spoke.

He lifted his hand a little bit and he said, "You see the stream, David. The traditions are like a stream, too, a stream that flows through the generations of Jewish people. You don't do this bar mitzvah for God, my grandson, you do it for your people in the past and in the future. . . . If there's no tradition, there's no people." . . .

I felt pretty lousy as we walked back up through the woods and into the house. Everyone was standing around the kitchen when we walked in. Ma looked at me as if the answer to some question were written on my face. Then she looked at Max. Then Dad looked at me. Then he looked at Max. Nobody said anything for a minute. Then Nana said, "Come, everybody come into the dining room."

Nana had baked a beautiful challa and it was sitting on the dining room table. It's a big loaf of bread shaped like a crown, which Jewish people eat on special holidays. We all gathered around the table while Grampa sliced the challa. Then we each took a piece. Nana walked around carrying a bowl of honey. We dipped our bread in the honey and everybody wished everybody else a sweet new year. Dad came over and put his arm around me.

"So did you have a nice walk with your grandfather?"
he said.

"I've had better," I said.

Dad squeezed me a little tighter. Grampa poured the
wine, and when everybody had a glass, Dad lifted his
high in the air. "To David," he said, "to David."

Tradition is the theme running through that scene. In fact,
it's a word and a theme that runs through the whole book,
the plots and the subplots. David is a Boston Celtics basketball
fan, as Gary was. And, during the course of the story he's
saying he doesn't believe in tradition, in particular the Jewish
tradition.

At one point, he goes to a Boston Celtics basketball game
with his uncle, and he looks up and he sees hanging from the
rafters all these banners that the Celtics won over the years
for championships. And his uncle says, "Yeah, they're a great
team. With a great tradition." David is a little surprised at the
use of this word *tradition*, and he says, "What do you mean?"
His uncle explains to him the winning ways of the Celtics is
also a tradition. David begins to see that tradition is not just
something he practices on Saturdays in the temple, it's something that occurs throughout his life on a number of different
levels, just as it occurs at a number of different levels throughout the book.

So what is the word for you? If you haven't figured it out
yet, don't worry about it.

Gary once told me he talked about this to author Marilyn
French. She wrote the novel *The Women's Room*. She said,
"I wrote about three hundred pages of my novel before I knew
what I was writing about. And then I understood. I was writing
about rage." Rage is what it was for her in that novel. What
is it for you? What's the theme? What's the controlling idea
throughout?

Figure that out, even if it changes as your book grows in
the organic way that books grow, and you will have an answer

to how to invent incident and subplot, what kind of view-points will work and what kind of overarching metaphor can be woven throughout the narrative that will underscore, sub-tly, the theme you're writing about.

In music, you have melody and you have harmony.

In writing, you have story and theme.

Theme is particularly relevant when it comes to creating subplots. The subplot in your narrative is not just something a character happens to be doing while the events of your narra-tive take place; it is something that relates to the plot in some structural way.

In short, the *story*, or plot, of your book is a sequence of events that are linked; the *theme* is what your book is about, the glue that gives your story a coherence and a unity of meta-phor and invention; *subplot* is usually one of the main means of demonstrating or showing (rather than telling) that theme without the need for some kind of editorial comment.

## SUBPLOT EMPHASIZES THEME

Remember the movie *48 Hrs*, with Nick Nolte and Eddie Murphy? We can guess that in the past, this cop has had a partner who somehow let him down, or maybe got killed. This cop has trouble working with partners. Then an officer is killed with the Nolte character's gun and he vows to catch the bad guys. Trouble is, he has to do it using the help of a partner—a criminal (Eddie Murphy) who used to hang around with the killer and knows his haunts and habits. So, in order to nail the bad guy, the cop arranges for the convict to get a forty-eight-hour pass out of jail, in the officer's custody.

So here we have a guy who is forced into a partnership with someone he doesn't much like, and who gradually, and grudgingly, gets to like and rely on the most unlikely of partners.

At various times throughout the movie, we see the cop in conflict with his girlfriend. They sleep together, but then he rushes off without much romance. They talk on the phone, but he's always got something more important he has to do right at that moment, so he puts her on hold, they fight, she hangs up on him. Clearly, his inability to work with partners extends to more than just police work.

This whole strand of narrative with the detective and his girlfriend is a subplot. It shows that the cop has a life beyond the confines of the main narrative, but it is not extraneous; it has a function that plays into the main story line. What is that function? It's to emphasize an important aspect of this guy's character even though it has no direct bearing on the pursuit of the killer.

Actually, no one else ever meets the girlfriend, although the new partners talk *about her*, briefly, as they slowly forge a bond. When the story finishes, and the two—together—capture (read kill, in this case) the bad guy, the girlfriend doesn't appear, so there is no scene resolving the conflict with her. Yet we really don't notice this or even feel bothered by it. Why?

Because audiences—including readers—instinctively understand that plots and subplots deliver "messages" about each other. So when, in the main story, we see Nolte's character finally learn to work in partnership and friendship with someone else, we don't need it to be spelled out for us that this will probably spill over into his personal life. If things worked out with the convict, the implication is that they will eventually work out with the girlfriend. So there's no need for a final subplot scene to underscore what we already know.

To emphasize what I said before: A subplot is not just a bunch of stuff that happens to a character during a slow part of the main narrative. It has a connection with the main narrative, in the same way that harmony enriches and embellishes the lyrical line.

## THE RELATIONSHIP BETWEEN PLOT AND SUBPLOT

Plot and subplot have a relationship: They come closer, they move apart, but they're never unaware of each other.

In Gary's Silhouette romance, *Share the Dream*, the main plot is, of course, the romance.

In the subplot, the protagonist, Carol, wants to spend more time and get closer to her sister, Bonnie.

So the sisters decide to go on vacation together. Not surprisingly (as this is a romance), Carol meets a fellow. When that happens, her success level goes up in the main plot because she moves closer to finding Mr. Wonderful. However, it moves *down* in the subplot, because she starts to neglect her sister in favor of Mr. Wonderful. When Mr. W appears to be married, Carol's potential success at achieving her goals in the main plot plummet, but now she can play Scrabble with her sister, so her success rate at achieving her goal in the subplot goes up.

It turns out it was all a misunderstanding over Mr. W being married, and he invites Carol to dinner. Now her success rate in the main plot is rising, but, uh-oh, she has to cancel a date with her sister to meet Mr. W, and her success rate in the subplot takes a nosedive as a result.

Of course, in writing, nothing is ever that pat, but I hope you get the idea that plot and subplot(s) interweave. They "braid," if you like.

## Subplot as an Echo of the Main Plot

Gary and Gail wrote a sequel to *Good If It Goes* called *David and Max*. The book is about David, a twelve-year-old Jewish boy, who helps his grandfather search for an old friend from a Nazi concentration camp. In the process, David learns about the persecution of the Jews in Germany in the 1930s and 1940s, the Holocaust and the terrible things that happened to his people.

It is, largely, a book about persecution. In other words, that's its theme.

But, there's a subplot that makes the book more playful, and more specifically designed for the young adult market it was written for. David likes to play basketball, but he's very short, and the other kids won't let him play. In effect, he is persecuted for being short. It's not a terrible thing. They're not vicious to him, but the theme of persecution is played out and developed in a more directly emotional way for David. It is something that directly affects him, and gives both him and the reader an inkling of what it must have felt like to live in his grandfather's shoes all those years ago, and, more importantly, it also helps readers grasp the awful enormity of what happened.

The connecting idea here, of course, is persecution and variations on that theme. In the main plot, there is the most wicked kind of persecution, based on bigotry, and in the subplot, the element is present in a more benign form: persecution of the short.

## Subplot as Contradiction of the Main Plot

A subplot can also run counter to an idea or statement in the plot. Do you remember the movie *King Kong*? A giant ape is captured and taken from his island home to New York City. He gets free and sets about roaring and ripping apart buildings in Manhattan.

Do you also recall how gentle and sweet he is with Fay Wray's character, the girl he falls in love with? That's a deliberately contradictory subplot that gives you a clue as to who the real villains are in the main plot, and it's a nice counterpoint harmony to the main story line's melody. Again, it's strength is that it emphasizes an important emotional element of the main story and explores a quality of the main character that plays into the story, by giving us a better understanding of who the ape really is.

The subplot can also be an internal element. Say a man is trying to conquer a mountain. That drama will be played out in an external, physical, and visual way.

But the subplot could well involve an internal, character-driven element, such as his efforts to conquer his fear or guilt, a staple motivation for a number of central characters in plays and stories from Shakespeare's *Macbeth* to Willy Loman in Arthur Miller's *Death of a Salesman*.

Ideally, even though an internally driven plot, it should, as much as possible, be dramatized in an external way, eventually preparing readers for the stakes and prizes that await the hero's attempted conquest of the mountain.

## A AND B STORIES

If you watch situation comedies, you'll notice that they always seem to have an A story (or main story) and a B story (or subplot).

When the scripts are well written, there will always be a connection between the two stories. In the A story, maybe young woman character number one is trying to get rid of a persistent suitor. This will be played with some humor and poignancy. In the B story, meanwhile, male friend number two is being hounded by telemarketers, and not being the confrontational type, he hits on an elaborate lie to explain why he doesn't want ten years' supply of "almost free" vitamin pills for "only" $59.95 per month for the next five years.

Two seemingly unconnected stories. But both are linked by theme. The theme, of course, deals with the way we reject people or, perhaps even more specifically, the white lies we tell in an attempt to avoid hurting someone's feelings and all the trouble such action can get us into.

Having figured out the theme, it is relatively simple to come up with a subplot to reflect the variations of that theme. So the subplot is clearly *not* chosen at random, nor does it involve an element in the character's life disconnected from the main story.

A subplot can also be a continuing dream, a persistent memory, a lingering romance, a major ambition, a pressing project, anything, in fact, that somehow resonates with or illuminates the main narrative, throwing a new light on it.

## WHAT'S PLOT AND WHAT'S *NOT*?

A plot is *not* everything that happens in your character's life from the moment the story begins until the point when it ends. Readers have no interest in when he eats his meals, what he eats, how he eats, when he goes to the bathroom, how many times, which hand he uses to wave good-bye to his family, etc. All these things may happen, but they are not relevant to your story. You must be selective in choosing the appropriate detail. This may sound easy and ridiculous put like this, but inexperienced writers attempting to reconstruct real events, be they for a historical book, a true crime account or some other genre, are faced with a very real version of this problem all the time. How do you determine what is plot and what isn't from the mass of facts and events that have been gathered?

A plot is a specific path of events that affect the outcome of your narrative. If an event doesn't affect the story, it shouldn't be in your narrative.

Let's assume that Randy is the main character in a true crime story, and even though he is only a mailman, he decides to bring his wife's killer to justice because the police have given up on the case.

In the course of this story, however, Randy meets Maria in Miami Beach. He's trying to forget about what happened to his wife, without much success.

Now he finds himself, almost halfheartedly, going out to dinner with Maria, mainly because he doesn't want to be alone, and Maria's a good listener and good company. Before he knows what's happened, he's kissing Maria good-night.

Despite his preoccupation with solving his wife's murder, Randy begins to date Maria and get on with his life. However, after dinner one night, she announces she doesn't want to see him anymore because his obsession with his wife's death isn't allowing her into his life.

Finally, having solved the mystery of who killed his wife—and mundanely it turns out to be a next-door neighbor who thought, mistakenly, Randy's wife was having a lesbian affair with *his* wife—Randy is able to persuade Maria to come back into his life, because now he can finally put to rest the memory of his wife and put Maria first.

## WHAT'S SUBPLOT AND WHAT'S *NOT*?

Connect the dots of this line of events, and you have a subplot about Maria that is, in this case, illuminating the emotional life (or lack thereof) of Randy, the main character. Nevertheless, the subplot is a different story, though connected to the first.

It is a subplot because of the following:

1. It occurs during the period of the plot.
2. It has some sort of connection to the plot. (In this case, Randy is releasing one woman from his life while gradually accepting another woman into his life.)
3. The subplot story line does not change the plot line but enhances it.

It's worth considering, however, that a subplot *can*, and often does, influence the course of the main plot. In our true crime story, for example, because Randy wanted a life with Maria, he made a conscious decision not to try and exact an "eye for an eye" revenge on his killer/neighbor, but to help in the guy's apprehension by the police. Without Maria's indirect influence on his life, Randy might have tried to exact a revenge that would have put him in jail for twenty years.

If, though, we were to think about this narrative in terms of fiction, another important element enters the picture. What if Maria was in cahoots with the killer? Her job was to romance Randy and divert him from achieving his goal of discovering and capturing the killer. At this point, Maria's story stops being a subplot of the main story line, even if she is still enhancing the emotional life of the main character, and her "subplot" becomes an integral part of the main story. Clearly, she has become one link in a chain of events that began with the murder of Randy's wife—and that now makes her part of the plot.

A subplot can be thought of as a sort of adjective that describes and enhances the noun that is the main plot. As a result, it doesn't include when Randy brushed his teeth, bought sauerkraut or turned on CNN. The subplot is not a collection of random events that somehow enhance the emotional life of the main characters; it is a specific path of events that tell a story.

## THE DYNAMICS OF A SUBPLOT

A subplot should have the same kind of dynamic structure as the main plot. It should have a goal, it should have conflict, and it should have a point of view, which is not necessarily that of the protagonist, though most often it will be. It also subtly alludes to the answer to the question, Does your character have a life beyond the confines of your story?

The subplot, however, should not be a more compelling story than the main plot. If you find this happening, it is probably a good idea to rethink what you're writing and decide whether you should either drop that subplot or revise your original idea for a book so that subplot becomes the main plot. Then the entire project needs restructuring and rethinking in this light. Don't bring a subplot into a plot that is already complicated. The object is not to bewilder or confuse your reader, but to enhance and heighten the reading experience through an understanding of the characters' lives and feelings.

So what's the right number of subplots?

The answer is, there is no set number. Short stories and articles rarely have any. Many novels don't have any, although two or three is also not unusual. A good rule of thumb, however, is no more than three.

The question should be, What is the function of the subplot? If, as we've discussed, it is about enhancing the emotional life of the main characters, unless you're working on an epic story, you probably only want one, on average, per major character.

## THE STAR OF THE SUBPLOT

The star of your subplot can be the star of your story or a secondary character. However, in any subplot, there must be at least one character who appears in the main plot. If you write a subplot in which none of the characters have any connection to what's happening in the main story, you haven't written a subplot, you've written a separate story. If you can remove a subplot without having any noticeable or subtle effect on your main story, that subplot shouldn't be there. It is a good way to look at how to edit your massive first novel of

2,000 single-spaced pages to a more professional and manageable 350-400 double-spaced pages.

Even linked short stories and novellas (stories longer than short stories but not long enough to qualify as novels), such as Raymond Carver's *Short Cuts* or Quentin Tarantino's *Pulp Fiction*, have a world and characters in common. Minor characters in one story strand become major characters in another. Such writing and plotting is the structural basis of many TV shows, such as *NYPD Blue*, *ER*, *Homicide*, *Star Trek: The Next Generation* and *Star Trek: Deep Space Nine*, and is particularly strong in multistar cast shows. Often a main plot line will be echoed by subplots involving regular cast characters that somehow amplify and enhance the main story line.

When should you start a subplot? Most commonly, subplots begin early in a book, usually within the first quarter or first third of the narrative. They rarely begin late. The function of the subplot to your main story line will determine many of these kinds of questions. Remember, one of the primary functions of the subplot should be to enhance and dramatize the emotional life of the main character in connection to the events of the main story.

## TO BEGIN OR NOT TO BEGIN WITH A SUBPLOT: THAT IS THE QUESTION

Quite often, as with Gary's *Share the Dream*, the subplot is a way of beginning a narrative. Remember, we said a story begins with an inciting incident, a first domino that knocks over a second and so forth. Structurally, you want to place that inciting incident where it will have the most dramatic impact. While the majority of stories should start with what kicks off the story, there are times when you delay the inciting incident until the end of the first chapter or the beginning of the second and you have to have something happening in the meanwhile. That something will be the subplot.

Suppose Greg is trying to get court permission to abort his wife Jennifer's pregnancy because she's in a coma from a car crash and the abortion will improve her chances for recovery.

The inciting incident for that main plot is going to be the car crash that puts his wife into a coma.

But if you decide to start with the car crash on page one, you risk not maximizing the emotional involvement of your characters with your readers because they don't know anything about the people in the story. You want readers to know and care about these people first, so you can begin with a subplot.

Perhaps the husband and wife have just concluded a verbal agreement to build a new house, one they desperately want. They are scrimping, borrowing and working like lunatics to get the money to pay for this house. Readers see the couple wandering around the property, talking with the real estate agent, the contractor, the architect; discussing the building's progress; making plans for designing and decorating the nursery, the kitchen, the garden, etc.

It's on the way home from one of these meetings that they drive around a corner and come face-to-face with a semi that is overtaking another semi on a bend. The husband has two choices: hope to survive a head-on collision with a Mack truck or pull off the road into the trees and take his chances. That's when he jerks the wheel and crashes the car into a tree, putting his wife's head through the windshield and into a coma, and plunging himself into a living hell of hard choices and personal recriminations. This is how you end chapter one.

Throughout the story of his decisions with his wife's health, readers still see the subplot of his dealing with the lawyers, real estate agents, contractors and bankers and perhaps running into the same bureaucratic mind-set he is encountering among the hospital professionals and the lawyers.

## HOW TO END THE SUBPLOT

When is the subplot over? The subplot ends—or at least it should—when the main plot of a novel itself ends. A subplot often ends before the main plot comes to its climax.

The most satisfactory ending to a story with a subplot is for main plot and subplot to climax at the same time, the conclusion to one also providing the conclusion to the other. This is *really* hard to do and doesn't happen often. When it does, though, you know you have a well-plotted story, because no matter what you invent, it seems to naturally fit right into the story you're telling and clicks with or enhances an existing element.

In your story about Greg and Jennifer, it might work, for example, to have a subplot that stars a character called Toni. Her husband, Richard, is the builder who is working on Greg and Jennifer's new house. When Richard discovers what's going on in Greg's life, he mentions it to Toni.

Toni becomes the personification of the antiabortionists who elect to protect the interests of the unborn child and block Greg's attempts to abort the baby and save Jennifer's life. But Toni is not a villain; she is a caring, well-meaning, religious woman.

Greg feels: Who are these people to barge into his life, after all the tragedy and heartache, and start telling him what he can and cannot do?

Toni and her group feel: How dare Greg arbitrarily play God and decide whether this unborn, defenseless child should be sacrificed for the sake of the mother? Doesn't Baby Doe have the right to exist, too? Toni and her group get the courts to award them guardianship of the unborn child.

One night, after drinking in a local bar, Greg walks into the car park and comes across a man and a woman having a violent fight in a car. Determined not to interfere, Greg walks away, despite the screams and shouts. However, his conscience brings him back, and he raps on the car window. Seeing the struggle still going on inside, but hearing only muffled sounds, he jerks open the door in time to see the man on top of the woman in the passenger's seat, strangling her. Greg pummels the man and pushes him off the woman, drags her into the car park and yells for help. The car drives off, wheels squealing. Finally, someone in the bar runs out and helps saying the cops have been called. To his surprise, however, the woman not only refuses to press charges against her companion, she berates Greg for interfering, saying it's his fault her man ran away and left her. Why didn't he mind his own business?

Returning to the hospital, Greg sees that while he may save Jennifer's life at the expense of the child's, it is unlikely she will ever be a shadow of the woman he married, if she even awakens from the coma at all. Objective advice is to deliver the child by cesarean and let Jennifer take her chances. To do that, however, Toni and her group have to agree to this course of action. Once the child is born though, ironically, guardianship returns to Greg as the child's blood relative.

Meanwhile, Toni, in her subplot, pursues custody of her kids and deals with the impending divorce from her husband. Richard feels she is an unfit mother because of what she has wrought on his family as a result of her antiabortion activities. Toni, through her interaction with courts, lawyers, and state agencies trying to protect her children from her, comes to terms with what happens when strangers interfere in your life in such fundamental ways. Where do people draw the line involving moral and ethical principles that force them to interfere in the conduct of others? The last scene will be Toni and Greg at Jennifer's bedside struggling to communicate and express themselves but not really finding the words that describe the depth of their feelings as Jennifer is wheeled out to deliver her baby.

It might be a useful exercise to try and invent several of the dramatic scenes that highlight the forward movement of this story, including the scene where Toni and Greg meet at the end and forge some sort of forgiveness of each other. The first question you need to ask is, What is the story's theme? The answer would seem to be involvement or interference.

It would also be useful to completely replot this story, exploring the possibilities of Jennifer's likely full recovery if the baby is aborted.

In the movie *The Fugitive*, as another example, when Kimble confronts and defeats Sykes, the one-armed man, in the subway train, it concludes the subplot about catching the man who killed Kimble's wife. But by this time, he knows Sykes worked for someone else—a doctor named Nichols who is also Kimble's best friend (or so he thought) and the man really responsible for Kimble's wife's murder. During the confrontation with Sykes, a cop gets killed. This ratchets up the emotional power of the climax with Nichols, because now Kimble has not only got Gerard hot on his heels, but the entire Chicago police force determined to shoot to kill because they think Kimble's a cop killer. In this case, the subplot has provided a springboard to an increased intensity in the climax.

In general, the structural sequence should be something like this: Subplot number two ends, then slightly more important subplot number one ends, then finally, in a grand finale, your main plot concludes.

It often doesn't work out that neatly, however.

In the movie *Diehard*, based on a novel by Roderick Thorp, in the main plot a bunch of commando-like thieves pretending to be terrorists take over a skyscraper. The thieves hold a bunch of people who were at an office party hostage long enough to pull off a robbery.

Bruce Willis is a cop named John McClane who finds himself on his own and at large, and he scurries around like a rat in the wainscoting, waging a guerrilla war against the thieves. His goal is to bring an end to the siege and rescue the hostages, one of whom is his estranged wife, played by Bonnie Bedelia.

In a subplot, a TV reporter outside the building has located McClane's kids and put them on TV, much to the dismay of their parents and also greatly enhancing the danger that McClane and his wife find themselves in. However, there's no way this subplot can end before the main story ends, because McClane would have to sneak out of the building, deal with the reporter and then sneak back in again, which would be a stupid thing to do, even if he could do it, and completely unbelievable. So the main plot has to end first, which it does with a great flourish of bombs and bullets and dead people. Now, with the main plot over, the audience's interest level has dropped dramatically as has their emotional involvement in the story. So the subplot has to end quickly and without subtlety. So what the filmmakers do is have McClane's wife march out of the building with her husband, spot the TV reporter, walk over to him and punch his lights out. It's an emotional tweak that works, even though it's an anticlimax to the main story, because viewers have been following the cop's wife on and off throughout the whole of this ordeal and it rounds off and concludes her story. The TV reporter subplot is thus really the wife's story, not McClane's, even though it affected his story line.

## A FINAL NOTE ABOUT SUBPLOTS

What subplots help to do is increase the emotional temperature of the main story, vary the main story's pacing and control the flow of plot information to the reader. One final point to consider is that while you won't kill off your principal character in your main narrative, you might well feel, for emotional impact reasons, you want to do that in your subplot (unless, of course, the star of the subplot is also the star of the book!).

The novelist Ed McBain, in his 87th Precinct police procedural novels, does this in several books in the series. Secondary characters in the squad room you've grown to know and care about unexpectedly find themselves in the middle of a shootout or a robbery, and they get hurt and sometimes killed as a result. It is an unexpected, emotionally shocking experience for the reader that helps underscore the main character's vulnerability. Danger can come at any time in police work, particularly when you least expect it.

## EXERCISES

1. Find out what you're writing about. Think about the theme of your current project. Don't worry if you can't come up with one immediately. The point is to be aware. Keep writing. The moment will come.

2. Develop a subplot for the following main plot: A marine comes home and learns that his son has been brainwashed into a religious cult. So the father joins the cult to try to find his son.

As you think about what might be an appropriate subplot for this book, look at some of the ideas in the main plot. In this case, some key topics are searching, military, religious cult.

What is it about those concepts that may suggest a subplot that echoes some of the ideas in the main plot, or runs counter to them, and will eventually link up to them?

*Chapter Eleven*

# Pace

Our literary agency receives, on average, about twelve thousand pieces of mail a year. Yes, you read that correctly—an average of one thousand unsolicited query letters, proposals, and manuscripts per month. About 95 percent of the material that gets sent to us is rejected.

Why? Because the vast majority of the manuscripts all have at least one mistake in common—the pacing of the story is off. About two or three in a hundred are paced too quickly. That is, the writer has rushed through his story, skipping over things, writing an extended synopsis in effect. About 95 percent of the rest, that is, the vast majority, are paced too slowly. There are setup scenes, unnecessary scenes establishing unimportant plot or character points, unnecessary words, scenes repeated from alternate viewpoints that didn't have to be repeated, unnecessary paragraphs, and so forth.

Alas, most writers simply write too many words that don't mean much or add much to the flow and progression of the story. Their stories, while often containing an interesting premise, quickly become bland, generic and, worst of all, dull.

Fixing this structural problem is what we're going to talk about in this chapter.

## MOVING CHARACTERS CLOSER TO THEIR FATE

You might recall that when we talked about writing scenes, we said that each scene needs to move the story forward. After you've written a draft or two of your story, look honestly at each scene in your manuscript and ask yourself, Do the characters in this scene somehow move inexorably closer to their fate?

If they don't, you have to rewrite the scene, or possibly get rid of it. You don't want anything in your book that is doing the same work twice. That is, you don't want a word, paragraph, sentence, or scene that is doing work already being done by another word, paragraph, sentence, or scene.

It may help, for structural purposes, if you think of your story as being divided up into *story events* and *other information*. Gary used to measure the progress of a student by taking her manuscript and underlining everything in the manuscript's first ten pages that he considered a story event, that is, forward movement, some sort of action the character was taking. Then, with a different-colored pen, he looked for and underlined everything he thought of as other stuff—description, background material, static stuff that didn't have any dynamic movement to it. You might take a break from reading this book now and do the same exercise to a scene from your manuscript.

What Gary found was that the student usually puts in maybe two, three, or four forward-moving story events—that is, story-progressing sentences—in as many pages. Then he took one of Robert B. Parker's Spenser novels and did the same exercise. (Actually, it could have been almost any well-published writer's work, but Gary was a fan of Parker's and chose him for that reason.) Gary found a ratio of four to one, that is, four sentences of information to one sentence of action. It might well be small movement, such as someone going for a Coke, but, while this shouldn't be thought of as a formula in any way, in general your book needs to be close to Parker's ratio. One out of five of your sentences should advance the story.

Let's take a couple of examples from other writers to see how the ratio stands up. Here's a passage from *The Rosewood Casket* (Dutton/Signet), by Sharyn McCrumb. The story event sections are underlined for emphasis:

Kayla <u>had awakened</u> to a quiet house. <u>She dressed herself</u> in tiny jeans and a red sweatshirt from her canvas suitcase and <u>went downstairs, calling out for her mother</u>, but all was quiet. Kayla <u>was not particularly disturbed</u> by this. Until recently, <u>her mother had worked changing shifts</u> at a twenty-four hour dry cleaners in Nashville, catering to people in the music business, who kept odd hours themselves. Since night shift child care was almost impossible to find, much less afford, <u>Kelley had dispensed with it</u> on the weeks she worked eleven to seven, reasoning that Kayla might as well sleep in her own bed, and that the money would be better spent on food and clothes for the child. Kayla was used to waking up alone. <u>She rummaged</u> through the refrigerator, and <u>found orange juice</u> and homemade jam. The bread was in a wooden box at the back of the kitchen counter, but <u>by dragging the chair</u> over to the counter, <u>she found that she could reach it</u> and the toaster beside it.

## DOES ANYBODY CARE?

Pacing, then, is about the speed at which you tell your story. There are several techniques you can use to effectively pace your story, including flashbacks, transitions and getting rid of all the unnecessary parts of your narrative—the stuff everyone skips in order to get to the good stuff, what happens next.

One of the things you want to think about in your writing at any given point in your manuscript is, Does anybody care? Are you writing something that has no humanity to it?

Here's an example from one of Gary's student's early work:

Sunrise began to paint its kaleidoscope of pastels on the desert of New Mexico. The cool August morning gave way rapidly to rising temperatures, and to the grey, violet outline of butte and cactus. These forms, hidden for hours in darkness, now appeared in changing hues

> of pink and orange. Step by step the sun's palette dis-
> tributed its gentle splendor onto a vast canvas of silvers.
> All night long, the man-made glare of white light shone
> from massive staging platforms and block shaped build-
> ings that made up section 4 of Holliman Airforce Base.
> The strong white dots from these lamps now became
> less and less intense as the sun set to work establishing
> its light and warmth over all of the base's 160 square
> miles.

OK, first problem, as we've discussed earlier: There's no
established viewpoint. It's pretty stuff, but there are no people
present. Who is doing all this observing? And because there
are no people present, there's no forward story movement.
The writing is static and boring. It's setting up a scene, but
there's no need to set up the scene this way.

> Joe Bloggs watched the shadows of dawn give way
> to the beginnings of a glaring, colorful morning in the
> New Mexican desert, as the sun's growing warmth took
> the chill out of the air over Holliman Airforce Base be-
> low him.

Now we've established in a sentence (if a touch purple-
prose-like, admittedly) what was not established in six sentences (actually more, because the example goes on like this for
a couple of pages). If you find yourself waxing lyrical like
Gary's student, writing a lot of pretty words but nobody is
doing anything, you are going to have to cut them. No one
cares. There's no emotional involvement.

Sometimes Gary would say this to writers and they'd say,
"Well, Gary, I saw something in a book I read, and it's the
same thing." They're talking about something they *think* they
saw.

Here's an example. It's the lead from Scott Spencer's book
*Endless Love*, which was one of Gary's favorite pacing examples. And with good reason. At first glance the passage may

appear to be something rather precious and pretty, even somewhat pretentious in its tone, but as you'll see, it would be a mistake to think that way. We'll go over this passage in some detail and examine how Scott Spencer paces his story:

> When I was seventeen and in full obedience to my heart's most urgent commands, I stepped far from the pathway of normal life and in a moment ruined everything I loved. I loved so deeply, and when the love was interrupted, when the incorporeal body of love shrank back in terror and my own body was locked away, it was hard for others to believe that a life so new could suffer so irrevocably. But now years have passed, and the night of August 12, 1967, still divides my life.

Despite the heavy-handed literary tone of this passage, it has the feel of movement to it. Why? Let's look at it again:

> When I was seventeen and in <u>full obedience</u> to my heart's <u>most urgent</u> commands, <u>I stepped far</u> from the pathway of normal life and in a moment <u>ruined everything</u> I loved. <u>I loved so deeply</u>, and when the love <u>was interrupted</u>, when the incorporeal body of love <u>shrank back in terror</u> and my own body was <u>locked away</u>, it was hard for others to <u>believe</u> that a life so new could <u>suffer so irrevocably</u>. But now years have passed, and the night of August 12, 1967, <u>still divides my life</u>.

There are eleven things happening in that passage (all underlined) all actions that foreshadow the story or move it forward. The passage is filled not only with active, action words, but words that bear directly on the story that is about to unfold in the coming pages.

## FORESHADOWING

Foreshadowing is something that comes through planning your story's twists and turns and through rewriting.

At its simplest, foreshadowing ties one seemingly unrelated

incident to another that occurs later on, making readers see that second event in a whole new light.

For example, suppose a detective is investigating a kidnapping. During the course of the story, the detective finds a brass button embossed with an anchor crest. This is a kind of foreshadowing if the button proves to be a material clue to who kidnapped the child. Say, for example, that later on in the story, the detective searches the child's uncle's bedroom and finds a blazer with a button missing. The button he found earlier matches the blazer's other buttons.

Perhaps the protagonist hates heights and has to struggle with his vertigo when he ventures onto a cliff face to recover the brass button. This makes the discovery of the button much more dramatic and sets up the solution of the mystery as well as a dramatic conclusion.

Let's assume the climax of the story takes place on a Ferris wheel. Because you foreshadowed the hero's fear of heights, the denouement has much more drama. Readers can see it coming and start to feel apprehension and then fear for the character even before the character starts to experience these emotions.

Even better, instead of searching the villain's bedroom, what if, at a fairground, the hero discovers who the villain is because the villain (still the child's uncle as you originally planned) wears his blazer with the missing button? Suppose a chase ensues that forces the protagonist onto a Ferris wheel where the villain has taken refuge in some manner.

The best structure is not a series of parallel, sometimes intersecting, lines, but coils. The story seems to swoop back on itself; however, it does not return to where it started, but instead arrives at another plane and heads in a logical (because of what has gone before), but unexpected direction (because of a different way of looking at those events). In some senses, writing a narrative can be thought of as posing and then solving a series of lateral-thinking problems.

Here's an example of what I mean: A man's car develops a flat tire in the middle of a teeming rainstorm. In the course of changing the tire, he knocks over the hubcap in which he's been keeping the wheel nuts, and they all roll down a drain, never to be seen again. Now, how does he get the wheel back on the car and drive safely home?

The answer is that he takes one nut from each of the remaining three tires and drives cautiously but safely home on four wheels fastened with three nuts each. Lateral thinking. It is one of the narrative storyteller's most potent tools when used properly. (If you are interested in reading more about this, check out the work of Professor Edward DeBono, who, in the 1960s and 1970s, wrote a series of books about lateral thinking.)

## TRANSITIONS

During Gary's video workshop it started to rain while he was giving a lecture outside. In order not to get wet, he had to hightail it into the house. The scene in the video then switched from Gary outside, trying to avoid getting wet, to Gary running inside from the rain.

As it happened, there were only a few minutes between each scene, but the passage of time between the two events could have been an hour, a week, even a year. The juxtaposition of putting one scene immediately after the other so it matches the details of the scene before suggests there is no serious lapse of time, just a change of camera viewpoint.

But suppose there had been a year in between Gary getting wet outside and resuming his lecture inside. How would a viewer feel if she were forced to sit and watch Gary tell her about everything he did during that period of time between scenes?

"Oh yeah," he'd say, "I dropped off at the plumbing supply store and got myself a few gaskets. And I ran into my friend Josephine. She's still doing pretty well, and we chitchatted about her mother-in-law for a while. Then I stopped off at the diner. Got myself a tuna fish sandwich," and on and on.

It would get pretty boring, wouldn't it? The reader isn't interested in what happened between the scenes; she only wants to know what happened in the scenes themselves. That's what relates to the story.

Your reader doesn't care about transitional material. She doesn't care what happened between events in the story. She cares only about what happened next—about the events. So you want to minimize the transitions.

## Scenes in Books and Movies

A transition in your writing is not unlike a transition in a movie. When you go to the movies, you see that something happens, quick cut, then something else happens. In writing, you need a bridge or two, something such as, "When they got back to Chicago," or, "Meanwhile, back at the ranch," or, "Twenty years later," or, "When Frankie arrived on Thursday"—that sort of thing. You're cueing the reader that you've gone to another time and place. And you've done it with a minimum of words and detail.

Here's an example of what you don't want to do: Lenny and Irving decide to hijack a bullion truck. In one scene, they get together and make the plan. That's kind of exciting because they have a disagreement about how best to hijack the truck. The next scene that's really important in the story is when they do the hijacking. Here's a sample bridging passage:

> "Tuesday morning, when the truck pulled into view in Lenny's rearview mirror, they put on their masks and got ready to rob it."

Unfortunately, lots of writers do something such as this:

> On Saturday, Lenny was still thinking about bullion hijacking. How many bags of cash would there be? he wondered. When he got to the rope factory, he avoided talking to his co-workers for fear of giving anything away. At lunch he didn't go to Danny's grill, the regular place where all the guys usually gathered, instead he

went to the Clifton Cafe. Should I order a bagel? he wondered. Naw, he thought. Instead, he ordered the grilled cheese sandwich on whole wheat toast and a glass of chocolate milk. Irving was all right, he thought, a nice guy, and sharp. When the five o'clock whistle blew at the rope factory, he went straight home. He turned on the TV and settled down to watch the Rangers game. When it was over he went to bed, but it was hard to sleep thinking about all that money, so he read for a while until he felt sleepy. Then he turned out the light, rolled over and eventually fell asleep.

You don't need to tell us every detail of a character's life. You're not writing his life, you're writing his story. And if he goes from Thursday to the following Monday with nothing important happening, readers understand he had a normal uneventful life. You don't have to waste time recounting it. No matter how much time or how much space is covered in the transition, you still need only a few words, one or two sentences.

Let's say you include a love affair in a science fiction novel. The lovers meet in 1997, and through some miracle of technology, they arrange to meet again in another twenty thousand years, and even then, it's on some planet six billion miles away. You simply write, "They met twenty thousand years later in a galaxy far, far away." A single sentence. You can see that readers wouldn't want to read about everything that happened in those twenty thousand years. The same thing goes for a couple of days. Readers don't want to have to read about everything that happens during that period of time either.

## The Reader Will Understand

What we're talking about are transitions in which the action that occurs is obvious for the reader and doesn't need to be covered. Nothing of importance, in story terms, takes place between the scenes. For example, if you've said that someone in a scene in Boston has to go to Chicago, it is sufficient to

write, "When Sammy got to Chicago." You don't have to include, "He left his apartment, he got in his car, turned on the
ignition, drove down the street . . ." The reader understands
all the steps that got Sammy to Chicago.

However, if something did happen during this transition
that needs to be explained, you need to acknowledge that to
the reader.

H. Rider Haggard, author of *King Solomon's Mines*, used
to write cliff-hangers for the *London Serials* monthly magazine
during the Victorian and Edwardian eras. In one of his stories,
he had a character called Ben. At the end of each installment,
Ben would be in a terrible calamity, and readers would wait
with bated breath for the next month's issue to see how Ben
got out of trouble.

At the end of one particular installment, poor Ben was at
the bottom of a twenty-foot pit, with no tools or weapons with
which to help himself and no one around to hear his cries for
help. Poor old Ben was in a pickle. Of course, all the magazine's readers sat around for weeks wondering, How's Ben
going to get out of this one?

Problem was, Rider Haggard was wondering the same thing.
When his deadline arrived, he still hadn't come up with a
clever way to get Ben out of trouble. Well, the next issue
arrived, and the readers eagerly turned to the start of the story.
To their amazement, Rider Haggard had written, "When Ben
got out of the pit, he went to London. . . . "

It isn't recorded what the reaction of the public was to this
solution, but you can bet that the vast majority of his readers
were very unhappy. Rider Haggard had tried to use a transition
to get himself out of trouble. You can't use transitions to do
that. No "with one leap he was free" kind of stuff. It's cheating, and you will seriously aggravate your readers to the point
where they may well fling your story across the room in disgust
and never pick up another book by you ever again.

If it is not obvious how your character got to be in the time
or place you're writing about during the transition, you need
to explain that.

## FLASHBACKS

One of the aspects of pace that troubles a lot of writers is flashbacks. How do I get my reader from the present into the past, then back again? The first rule of flashbacks: If you can possibly avoid a flashback, don't put it in.

There is nothing literary about a flashback, and nothing really arty about it. It is usually clumsily handled and an annoyance to readers. Make certain you need one before you write it.

However, there are times when you do need flashbacks. It's not necessary, for example, to always tell your story in a chronological fashion. Certainly, you need to structure it that way in a story synopsis, but you don't have to tell it that way.

The key to writing a good flashback is to lead the reader gracefully through the transition into the past and bring him back through the same door you used to get into the past. What do I mean by that?

Say you have a character, a woman, who's in her forties, and she's just gotten some terrible news: Her husband is dead from a car accident. You have this scene where she receives this tragic news and she begins to cry. She sits on the couch, and her beagle, Buster, comes over to comfort her. She begins to think about how six years ago her husband first brought her Buster as a puppy.

So, as in real life, you're using a present-time catalyst, in this case Buster the dog, to trigger a memory that will take readers into the past. You begin the flashback sequence with,

> "It had been a lovely spring day when George came through the door holding the perfect birthday present, a puppy."

*Had been* is the past perfect tense. You use it once, maybe twice, to get readers six years into the past. Once there, however, you use a regular narrative past tense.

You can do whatever you want in that flashback. It can last through one scene or for the rest of the book. It doesn't matter. Readers move forward from that point as you relate the things she did with her husband and with Buster and the places she went—whatever you want to cover. The important thing is, when it's time to come back to the present, you say something such as,

> "And now, holding Buster, she knew it would never be that way again. She put down the dog, stood up, and walked out of the room."

When readers see the dog again, they remember, Ah ha, we were in a flashback, and now we're coming out of it. Buster was the door through which we went and which we came back. The catalyst doesn't have to be an object, but it must be something memorable, perhaps an unusual word or an inflection, whatever is likely to spark a memory. That's what flashbacks are: the dramatized best bits of a character's memory.

William Goldman, in a novel called *The Color of Light*, has a character called Chub on a college campus:

> Late on a late spring afternoon Chub saw a girl . . .

She turns out to be someone he knew six months before, and we're into the flashback and we see his relationship with this girl, and after several scenes, Goldman brings us back to the present by saying:

> And now, late on that late spring afternoon Chub wondered if he should speak to her again.

She is the catalyst that triggers the memory of the past, and the phrase "late on a late spring afternoon" becomes the doorway to the past that takes us into the flashback and eventually brings us back.

We remember we were in a flashback and are brought immediately back to that college campus where he began the story. That is a properly done flashback.

In Oscar Hijuelos's 1990 Pulitzer prize-winning novel, *The Mambo Kings Play Songs of Love* (Farrar, Strauss & Giroux), the main thrust of the novel's narrative is set up as a flashback by the opening paragraph:

It was a Saturday afternoon on La Salle Street, years and years ago when I was a little kid, and around three o'clock Mrs. Shannon, the heavy Irish woman in her perpetually soup-stained dress, opened her back window and shouted out into the courtyard, "Hey, Cesar, yoo-hoo, I think you're on television, I swear it's you!" When I heard the opening strains of the *I Love Lucy* show I got excited because I knew she was referring to an item of eternity, that episode in which my dead father and my Uncle Cesar had appeared, playing Ricky Ricardo's singing cousins fresh off the farm in Oriente Province, Cuba, and north in New York for an engagement at Ricky's nightclub, the Tropicana.

This was close enough to the truth about their real lives. . . .

The keys to the flashback here are "years and years ago when I was a little kid" and "When I heard the opening strains of the *I Love Lucy* show I got excited because I knew she was referring to an item of eternity."

The whole passage is infused with a sense of remembrance ("It was a Saturday afternoon . . . years and years ago. . . ."), then there's a subtle shift to a more immediate present ("When I heard the opening strains of the *I Love Lucy* show I got excited. . . ."), then the "teasing" flashes of hindsight recollection that will become important as the narrative develops (". . . that episode in which my dead father . . ." and "This was close enough to the truth. . . ."). The use of tenses is very important in the flashback, and it is one of the reasons they are deceptively difficult to write well. If you're not careful, you can tie yourself and your readers in knots figuring out past, present and future in the narrative.

Some of the most intriguing examples of the use of flashback are in Ambrose Bierce's famous short story "An Occurrence at Owl Creek Bridge," about a Civil War soldier about to be hung from a bridge; and William Golding's *Pincher Martin*, about a drowning sailor. Both use the same conceit, that is, a flashback of the main character's life at the moment of his death. Perhaps the most complexly successful use of flashback that's worth studying is Muriel Spark's *The Prime of Miss Jean Brodie*, which ranges in time from the 1930s to the 1960s. A uniquely intriguing example is Harold Pinter's play (and movie) *Betrayal*, which tells the story of a love triangle *backward* in time. This was also used to powerful effect by J. Madison Davis in the novel *Bloody Marko*, and by Martin Amis in *Time's Arrow*.

## ACTION

This is the smallest building block you use as you construct your narrative. Don't be afraid to write a sentence about small actions. "He sat down in the chair." That's fine. "He stood up. He buttoned his shirt." They're all fine. You don't have to feel as though they're too trivial to write about. Readers can see them. There is movement. But make sure there is at least one new piece of information in each sentence.

So you might write, "He sat down and picked up his pen." That's fine. But what you don't want to write is a sentence that adds no new information or movement to the story, such as, "He sat down, he picked up his pen, it was black, it had a silver clip, it was made up of two pieces."

What you've done is rewrite information readers already know. They know there is a pen, and that's all they need to know—unless the specific information about the pen is important to the plot in some fashion.

The reverse of that is pushing the pace of the sentence too fast and omitting something: "He sat down. The cigarette tasted fine." The problem is, you forgot to have him take out the cigarette and light it: "He sat down. He lit the cigarette. It tasted fine." One action after another. They're little steps. But they're steps forward.

Another thing you want to think about in the matter of pace and little actions is the order in which you tell them. What you want to think about is something called stimulus and response. Here's an example:

> Shirley smashed into the chair in the living room. Ivan had just punched her in the face. That's the last time you'll hurt me, she thought. There was a lamp in the corner. Ivan ducked as the lamp came flying toward him.

What's happened here is that the writer has a pretty clear set of images about what is happening in this scene, but unfortunately, she's also assumed that the readers are as familiar with what is going on as the author is.

From the readers' perspective, however, they first saw Shirley fall down. *Then* they saw Ivan hit her. Later on, the readers saw Ivan duck, and *then* they saw a lamp come flying through the air. Get the problem? You need to be aware of both the literal sense of what you write and the sequence with which you write it. Writers often say things such as "'You're a real pest,' he growled nastily." It would be much better to write, "He growled nastily, 'You're a real pest'." Now readers have a clue *ahead of time* on how to read what's coming next.

Readers get information one step at a time. They don't read to the end and then go back. So, you should have written this:

> Ivan punched Shirley, and she fell down and smashed into the chair. That's the last time you'll hurt me, she thought. She glanced around the room, saw the lamp, grabbed it and threw it at him. He ducked.

That's the order in which all those actions take place. Every sentence is a stimulus for another action. So make sure you write sentences and actions in their logical order.

## DESCRIPTION

Imagine for a moment that you're downtown on a rainy afternoon. You come upon an interesting old theatre on a side street. You walk inside and take a seat in the fourth row. The stage is bare, poorly lit, nothing terribly attractive to look at. After a moment, the actors come out and begin to read their lines. Perhaps there's a scene where they're sitting at a card table. What they have to say is witty, compelling, and interesting, and you're getting caught up in the story.

While you're seated, the stage begins to get decoration. Like magic, costumes appear on the actors. Lights come up to illuminate all that is going on. Now the scene has been enhanced. The lights, the costumes, the set and props are all adding to your experience. The story becomes more compelling. What the characters have to say is more interesting, more vivid. It's all more real to you. You're having a real good time, caught up in this play.

But what's going to happen if at some point the actors decide to leave the stage? How long are you going to sit looking at an empty stage? Not very long I imagine. And that's what description in the narrative is all about.

Remember, description is subject to viewpoint. In other words, it's a function of who is doing the seeing and how he is feeling.

Description is a slave, not a master. It enhances what you're doing, but it's not there for its own sake, just as a decorated stage doesn't have much interest until the actors arrive to perform their parts.

The most important thing to remember about description is to keep it short. For some reason, when writers start out, they fall in love with description. They give paragraph after paragraph of sunrises and sunsets and stars and moons. Description should be sprinkled on like salt, not smeared on like butter. A little bit goes a long way.

## EXERCISES

1. Go through five or six pages of your work and underline every sentence in which you can honestly say there is some action, some movement forward in the story. It may be a small movement, such as someone going to the refrigerator. Everything else you don't underline will be other information, exposition and so on. Now go back and underline that in a different color. The ratio should be something on the order of five to one. Don't worry about that ratio, but if you have twenty or thirty sentences where there's no action, your story is moving too slowly and you should pick up the pace.

2. Take a scene you've written, and go on an adjective and adverb hunt. Mercilessly delete every single adjective and adverb you find. After you've done that, read the passage aloud. You should notice that the thing you tried to describe is still there. The reader still sees it. The pace of the whole scene picks up. After you've read the scene out loud to yourself, you can afford to put back some adjectives—but just a few. Look instead for active words you can use. Books don't *lie* on the table, for example, they're *stacked*.

*Chapter Twelve*

# Structure and Rewriting

One of the best analogies for writing is carpentry. Carpentry is about craft, an awareness of how things fit together snugly and seamlessly, an appreciation of the aesthetics of various types of wood (in the same way writers have a love for, and interest in words) and the harmonizing of the creative instinct with the mundane pragmatism of just measuring, shaping and fixing together pieces of wood.

While carpentry is a great analogy for writing, one of the best analogies for *rewriting* is the concept of shaping your words and ideas the way you would use a chisel, a plane or sandpaper to smooth and sculpt those pieces of wood into a seamless, graceful whole.

Writing is not just an attempt to get down on the page the "movie" that's going on inside your head. Writing involves editing and shaping and polishing the images and scenes of that movie until the words on the page convey *exactly* what you see when you close your eyes and watch and listen as your characters interact.

## FOCUSING ON WHAT'S IMPORTANT

One of the great problems of rewriting and self-editing is cutting, particularly when what has to be deleted is terrific writing, perhaps some of the best you've ever done. Remember, the higher calling is not the ambition to be a writer but to become a storyteller. Concentrating on what is important to the story—whether for a piece of fiction or narrative nonfiction—will help resolve many writing-related problems, such as what to cut and what to keep, what viewpoint to use, etc.

Writing is about grace and clarity of vision. It's about making sure the image in your head is on the page exactly as you imagine it. It's about rewriting—and rewriting is not easy, but it can be fun.

Some people overwrite on the first draft, getting down masses of words and images, and then they begin to pare away the garbage from the gold until the image shines through. Others put down mere skeletons of their ideas, and then having gotten down on the page some suggestions of what they want, they return to them and start to put muscle and then flesh on those skeletons until the images in the scenes stand firm and clear. Whatever works for you is what you should do.

Everything you learn about writing, whether it's from tapes, courses or books such as this, doesn't have to be applied in the first draft. In fact, it's unlikely you'll get it down in the first draft. Those initial words on the page are just a starting point. Now the work begins. Two drafts, three drafts, four, five, it doesn't matter. Write as much as it takes. Just remember it all has to be done by the time the manuscript is ready to be shipped to an agent or an editor. All the rules and suggestions in this book and elsewhere are just aids to help you figure out whether you've missed something important in creating your book, something that might get in the way of getting you published.

When you begin to write the first draft, don't question yourself, don't judge yourself, don't have this little guy on your shoulder passing comment as you work. Let it all come out as it will. Sure, some of it will look stupid afterward. So what? No one else will see what you've written. If you judge yourself too harshly too early on, you're going to miss out on some good creative stuff.

As you become more experienced, you'll learn to look for things in the creation of your drama, and the more you prepare ahead of time, the easier some of this will become. Try and recall what it was like the first time you sat behind the wheel of a car and started to drive on the streets. Remember all the things you seemed to have to do at once? Look ahead, look behind, check the sides, watch your speed, watch the road, watch the other cars, watch the rear mirror—it was endless, or so it seemed. Now you drive and do these things and don't think twice about them. They are things you do instinctively. Writing habits are the same.

One of the problems authors of both fiction and nonfiction face is that they struggle to be original, thinking that being original means flouting the guidelines of what readers expect when they go into a store and buy a book. (We discussed this a little in the chapter on genres.) This mistake, more than almost any other, marks the unpublished writer from the professional.

Remember the example we used of the romance novel with the title *Slasher From Hell*? Authors do the same kind of thing more often than many realize. They mix third person with first person, violate point of view or unity of time and place and so forth. However, they don't often read successful books that do that—for a reason. It's hard to pull off. What these inexperienced writers are doing is confusing *what* the story is with *how* you tell it. The story is not what happens, *but to whom it happens*.

## DEVELOPING YOUR STYLE

One of the primary things you should look for when reviewing your first draft is appropriateness of style.

Style isn't strictly a structural thing, so we haven't spent a lot of time on it in this book. The best style comes from reading and absorbing the work of strong writers. Who is a strong writer? There are plenty of books, writing courses and book reviews that will give you suggestions about who would qualify.

Writers are like actors. Different actors can play the same character and yet bring to the role an individual interpretation that is distinctive. What's more, while that actor's voice and style singles him out in a role, both may well vary from character to character and role to role as needs fit. In your case, as a writer, your voice on the page, your style, may well vary a little from story to story. Not only is that good, it is probably worth striving for in a subtle way. Try to fit the voice to the story if you can.

The most important place to start is to make sure you're using active words saying things in a positive way. Ask yourself, Is this sentence as powerful as it can be? Does every word carry its own weight? Am I saying what I mean simply and clearly? Can what I wrote be misunderstood? Does it have a literal meaning that is mocking the sense of what I'm trying to convey? Reread the early chapter on genre, where I talked about making sure your book has an appropriate title, one that fits in the book's genre, and that it uses language appropriate to that genre. The best way to know what's appropriate is to be intimately familiar with the genre you're writing in.

The rewriting process is where you will start to check for those sorts of thing.

Look at the beginning of the book particularly. Ask yourself, Have I begun with a character in a situation? Not with a lot of background or setup or description, but by plunging straight into the story and the situation. Remember, your audience reads to see how the main character gets out of the situation she finds herself in, how she solves the problem or the dilemma she is faced with. That's what catches readers and makes them care, forces them to turn the page.

You have to grab your reader from the outset. Editors want to find something good in what they read, but they don't have the time to spend wading through fifty or sixty pages of setup before the story begins. Compel readers to go on this journey with you by making them care about the people in your story and the situations they get themselves into and out of.

## Beginning and End
Once you look at the beginning of the book and make sure it grabs readers' attention, check the ending. What's resolved?

A lot of writers say, "I don't know how to end my book."

That's what all that early planning is for. But if you're still in trouble, go back and look at those first pages. Nearly every storys has the seed of its ending planted within the first chapter or so. If you're not sure what I mean by that, check out the movie *The Fugitive*. Almost everything you need to know about the solution to the puzzle in that movie is shown before the opening credits are finished.

In your first pages, you should create a problem, show something coming into a system and upsetting a status quo, and that's exactly what you try to undo by the end of the book.

Look at your book's last chapter and ask yourself, Does this resolve something that was begun way back at the beginning of the book?

If it resolves something that was begun in a chapter or two before the end, you're probably writing in an episodic way. Make sure the ending of the book relates to the beginning of the book.

When you look at the scenes you've created in your narrative, make sure there is something happening. You don't want a bunch of talking heads and no action. Make your characters *do*, not *say*, as much as possible. Is there an inciting incident for the scene? Does it have a goal, in terms of the overall movement of the narrative? Is there a reason for the scene at all? Where does the opposition come from? There should always be some conflict, an obstacle, a problem that has to be overcome.

Gary's mantra to his students was, "Conflict, conflict, conflict." It's the best advice.

## Description and Viewpoint

Look at your description. Ask yourself, Have I written three paragraphs of description that just sit there like lumps in gravy? If so, get rid of them. Remember, delete the bits everyone skips to get to the next piece of the story movement. Ideally, the description should be active, it should move the story along in some way. It should always be seen through a character's eyes, not the author's.

Check your viewpoint. Did you switch viewpoint in the middle of a scene? Ask yourself, Have I switched viewpoint too often? Have I used more viewpoints than I need?

Keep your transitions short. All you need is one or two passages to get you from A to B: "Meanwhile, back at the ranch . . ." "Later that day . . ." Keep it simple.

As you go through your manuscript, make sure that on every page there is conflict, people at odds with each other, with the world around them, with themselves. If there's no conflict, the reader's attention starts to drift from the page and the passage is not working.

Look for all these things during the rewrite. Don't worry about having them all present in the first draft. The important thing is to get it all right by the last draft. Keep in mind that words, like clay, are malleable. You can destroy them, erase them, rework your images and scenes until they look exactly the way you want them to look and sound and feel. The key, of course, is to have a clear idea of where you are going and what you want from your creation.

Writing is not a science, it's a craft, and you work at it and work at it until it starts to make sense. You push it and prod it and pull it and tweak it and polish it, until finally, almost miraculously, what is going on in your head starts to take shape on the page for all to see and read.

## FORM FOLLOWS FUNCTION

When we're indoors, we know the roof is not going to fall on our heads because we know the place was constructed carefully. Unfortunately, because of poor planning, sometimes the roof falls in on the beginning writer's head, metaphorically anyway, because he didn't construct his book with enough care and forethought, and he ends up sitting in the middle of a pile of rubble.

Of course, that's not going to happen to you because you're going to learn how to do it correctly. The building blocks—

beams, bricks and mortar, walls, shingles—for your book are scenes, exposition, half scenes, bridging passages, sequences, chapters, sections, actions, and so forth.

Chapters deserve a special mention. That's because they really don't have the same kind of rules about what is dramatically correct as some of the other components. Drama, action and exposition have specific definitions. Chapters, on the other hand, are whatever the heck you say they are.

Gary once wrote a proposal for a novel for which the publishers wanted the first two chapters as a sample of the rest of the book. But he had written a thirty-page chapter. He didn't feel like doing any more, so he went back to page 15 and broke the chapter in the middle.

Now this, in fact, works better for the reader than one long chapter, so far from being an act of sloth on Gary's part, it was an instinctive recognition that the pacing of the book could be picked up, if only by a little judicious restructuring of how the material was presented. It worked, because in our fast-moving, MTV-music-video-oriented, thirty-second-sound-bite, TV-advert-influenced world, readers like to know there are places to take a breather before plunging back into your imagined world, even if they don't use them all. Think of the fifteen- to twenty-page chapter length as the equivalent of rest stops along a parkway.

A chapter *can* be anything. The narrative itself *can't* be anything. *What* your narrative is begins with your synopsis and plot list. *How* it's put together is concerned with the kinds of drama you invent for your scenes, the action you put in them, the kind of language you use, the tone of the piece and so on.

Without all of these elements working together and in deliberate harmony, your narrative will not have structure.

## NARRATIVE STRUCTURE
### Sequence
The sequence is the basic level of narrative structure. A sequence is just a series of related scenes. Often, two or three

scenes will make up a chapter. So a sequence is *not* a chapter because, remember, a chapter can be anything you want it to be. *But*, a chapter can be a sequence. Confused?

Here's an example: In a romance, you may have a "falling in love" sequence. This may extend over a couple of chapters or just one.

Woman meets man. Woman has nice romantic dinner with man. Woman goes to man's cottage on the beach for late night wine. Romance blossoms.

This is followed by the "disappointment" sequence. Woman finds out man is a suspected murderer. Woman finds out man has an ex-wife who still wants him. Man tells woman he's taken a job in Brazil with the World Wildlife Fund.

The point about being aware of structure is not so much that you should think analytically when you're writing your first draft, but that when you come to revise that first draft, you have the tools at your command to see the overall shape of how the narrative is building and how it should be shaped, shored up and polished.

Go through your draft and look at each scene. Ask yourself, Is this in a sequence? Do these scenes relate to each other, or does this particular scene actually relate to a sequence I've put earlier or later in the book?

You'll discover that you may well have written some scenes that either are out of place and should be moved around or can be discarded.

## Exposition

Exposition is information. It's all the other "stuff" in your book that does not move the story along, but explains it. And because it explains or editorializes, exposition does work in the narrative similar to how adjectives and adverbs work in sentences: It enhances and clarifies. The right piece of exposition, like the correctly chosen adjective, can be powerful and effective. Used poorly, it becomes a crutch to the writer, preventing him from developing an otherwise imaginative way of delivering this information—if it's needed at all—an anchor retarding the forward momentum of the narrative and something that dilutes the emotional power of the story.

Some information, such as the background of characters and so forth, which we can define as information we need to know but isn't exciting, has to be in your narrative somewhere.

There are a couple of things to remember about exposition. First of all, don't give expository material, that is, information, until it is needed. For example, if, in scene three in your book, Julia meets Louise and you tell something about Louise's background, say that she used to be a policewoman but had to leave the force because she had an affair with the chief of police, wait until readers get into that scene with Louise before you give the information about her that's needed to fully understand the nuances of what is happening in that scene.

Second, as much as possible, try to get the exposition into scenes, or begin the scene before you give the exposition. What do we mean by that? Well, instead of saying, "Emily was a short Italian woman with long black hair, and on Monday she went to the personnel office to get a job as an assistant," do it this way: "On Monday, Emily arrived at the personnel office. She was a short Italian woman with long black hair."

The distinction is that by putting her in the personnel office first, that is, by setting a time and place, you frame the picture and the scene and make it easier to see Emily as a short Italian woman in a personnel office. Otherwise readers see her floating around, somewhat amorphously in space.

An even better way of tackling this information is to try and introduce it naturally into the scene through some piece of dramatic action. For example: "On Monday, Emily arrived at the personnel office. She took a chair in the corner and waited for her name to be called, and was rather embarrassed to realize that sitting down, her feet did not quite touch the floor. She began to feel like a midget. Unconsciously she used one hand to constantly sweep back her long black hair as it fell over her shoulders."

Note that we haven't mentioned she's Italian yet. Why? Because readers don't need to know that until something in the scene happens that will make it important. Then we'll figure out a way of introducing that important piece of information, just before we need it.

## Half Scenes

A half scene is something that's midway between a scene and exposition. There comes a time in your narrative when you want to give some exposition but you also want to give the flavor of a time or a place and so you mix the two.

It's most commonly used when you have something that's important for the reader to know but not important enough to devote a whole scene to. Here's an example: In Gary's novel *Baffled in Boston*, Scotty, the protagonist, goes to the police to check out the accident report on his friend Molly's hit-and-run death because he suspects she's been murdered. But it wasn't important enough to write a whole scene about. So, while Scotty is waiting to meet another character, Gary wrote this half-scene:

> The morning after my talk with Wayne, I had crowned myself sleuth and had driven into Boston to meet with the police officer who was investigating the hit-and-run case. He was an eager young fellow, Norman McCallow or McGowran or some such name, and he told me what I already knew: There was virtually no chance of catching the driver.
>
> "They don't leave calling cards," he said. When I told him about the message on my answering machine he pulled out the accident report again to see if there was something that he had missed. Nothing.
>
> "As you know," he said, "we can't start a homicide investigation on something like that." He said, "As you know," a number of times and it was obvious he knew who I was—or more accurately, who I had been, and still thought of me as a writer of true crime books. I left the police station that day with no new information except the names of four witnesses to the incident. One

witness had been hypnotized by a police psychiatrist
but the hypnosis had unlocked no forgotten memories.

It's a half scene because it's basically Scotty telling us a memory. But there's a little bit of dialogue, and the scene is made to come alive a little bit through dramatization.

## Action

The next level of structure is action. Action is simply what movement occurs in a sentence. "He walked into the room" is an action. "He sat down in the chair," is an action. "He folded his hands" is an action. "He said, 'I really don't care if you like me or not,' " is an action.

The point is to keep these actions happening and make sure there is a new action in every sentence. We discussed this in some detail in the chapter on pacing, so if you're still unsure, reread that chapter.

## EXERCISE

1. Take out some of your writing and find a scene, find a sequence, find an action, find each of the elements we've discussed in this chapter. Identify them, make a list and start becoming aware of the elements that make your narrative sound in form and forward moving in motion.

# Chapter Thirteen

# Fourteen Steps to Writing Your Story

Gary was never one for formulas, and neither am I, so it's important to bear in mind that what we have been talking about in this book is just *a* way of writing narrative, not *the* way.

I presume you're reading this book because you're having problems with "this novel-writing business" or a nonfiction idea is obsessing you in some way.

The point is, you'd like to write a book, either fiction or narrative nonfiction, but you just can't figure out how best to get started. Gary and I hope we have given you some clues and managed to switch on some lights and open some doors to reveal things you might not have noticed before.

Writers are an idiosyncratic bunch—probably all a little nuts when push comes to shove. Who else would shut themselves away in a little room, when everyone else is having a great time in the summer sun, and stay cut off from the rest of the world just so they could re-create visions of that world on paper?

Once those visions come into focus, writers try to capture them, to grasp the ideas behind the visions and wrestle with whatever angels or devils appear to impede the progress of creativity or seduce the writers into going somewhere else and distract them from their visions. Writers persevere. They try to massage those ideas into stories, and then try and use words— those notoriously slippery eel-like things—to commit those stories to paper. Surely sane people would not do all that.

## "NO" WILL ONE DAY BECOME "YES"

For that reason, writers are not likely to all do things the same way. Successful writers, artists, musicians, athletes, whatever are all, somewhere in their makeups, obsessive, dogged, won't-take-no-for-an-answer types—and *no* is a word you will hear a lot when you first start out as a writer. But it isn't a no about *you*, it's a no about *that particular piece of writing*. So learn from it. Keep trying and experimenting until you start hearing yes. Work at your craft long enough and with enough diligence, and you *will* hear that wonderful little word one day.

A lot of times when you're starting out, it's useful to have someone say, "Do it this way," if only so you can reject that way in favor of a better one you've figured out for yourself. That's absolutely OK. Whatever works for you is what you should be doing.

Writing is not a religion. There are no real rules, there is no catechism. We all learned what we do by *doing* it, over and over again until we got it right. What does that mean? It means we kept writing and submitting and listening to what those who were published bothered to say about our work until we started to get published. Until you're published, you're not always the best of judge of your own work.

If you find a way that works for you (and I mean that get's you published, and published regularly), ignore everything we've said in this book. The funny thing is, though, if you do get to that enviable position, chances are, you'll probably find what you're doing is a variation on the principles we've outlined in this book. But that's all they are—principles. Here then, in a nutshell, are fourteen important steps that should help keep you on track with your manuscript.

Note that steps one and two are interchangeable. You can do either one first.

## THE FOURTEEN STEPS

1. Write a synopsis of your story detailing in some fashion its beginning, middle, and end. It should be at least two pages long single-spaced.

2. Write a master plot list for your main character, including inciting incident, goal, opposition, and so forth.

3. Do the same thing for all your other important characters. A character should be in your story because he has a reason to be there. They must have a reason of their *own* for being in your story, not reasons *you* want them to have. Characters have a terrible habit of taking over sometimes, so be aware, be wary, be alert, be flexible, listen to what they say to you. They may be trying to tell you something that will improve your story, but they may also be asking for bigger roles in your story than they really deserve.

4. Write a backstory for each major character. Construct a biography filling in some of what you've discovered from step two. It doesn't have to be long, perhaps only a page or two, but you should know something about where these people came from, both literally as well as figuratively. That way, you know where they intend to go and you have a good idea how to put obstacles in their way with clues as to how they will overcome these obstacles.

5. Get some $3 \times 5$ index cards (or whatever size you like). Each of these cards will represent a scene in your book, and on it you will write the name of the scene or whatever key word you can think of that will help you fix and remember this scene; the inciting incident for the scene; the goal of the scene; the strategy for the scene; and the opposition and movement in the scene. Is the main character closer or further away from his ultimate goal in the story as a result of this scene? Remember, this is just a shorthand for yourself. You might want to color code your cards. Use different colors for dream sequences, different characters' viewpoints, subplots, etc. This will result in a kind of random access overview of your plot and the movement of your story. If you think of another scene in your story, write it up and stick it in the pack of cards wherever you think it will work best. Not happy with the sequence of events? Shuffle the cards until they make sense, then reorder your book accordingly.

6. Get another set of cards in a different color, and fill in any

necessary exposition or "other stuff" on them. For example, if your character gets a job working in a bakery for part of the novel, use this card to outline or fill in the information you may need to convince readers they are in a bakery and in the company of bakers. Readers don't need to attend a seminar on the subject. All you need to do is convince them these are real bakers working in a real bakery. Come up with two or three really telling observations about bakers and their world. That should do it.

7. Before you start writing, think carefully about scene one. Try to see it in your mind's eye; visualize it and conceptualize it *before* you sit down to write. In fact, try to do that with all your writing. Try to develop the habit of going to the word processor when you've got something to say, rather than sitting there staring at a blank screen suffering from some sort of creative constipation. Imagine the scenes of your book in your mind's eye first, then go to the word processor with a purpose. Who is going to do what to whom? What's the force of the scene? The thrust of the scene? Have you started it as close to the action as you can? Have you ended it as soon as the action in the scene is over? Writing is about *thinking*. Good writing is about clarity of thought and interesting ideas written so simply a teenager can quickly grasp them.

8. Got that scene bubbling nicely in your imagination? Then rush to the word processor and write the first draft of scene one. Write it in a blazing heat of creativity. Do whatever it takes to get it down. It doesn't matter if it's good, bad, or indifferent, it just has to exist on the page in some form. You can shape it and polish it later.

9. Now, in more calm reflection, print scene one and start working on it with a pencil or pen in preparation for creating draft two of scene one. Go through the scene for flaws in logic. Have you made assumptions the reader won't understand? Do events lead logically from cause to effect; have you had a quick look at the literal sense of what you've written? Is it obvious and clear what is happening, who is talking to whom and so forth? Now, take a break and pat yourself on the back. The

worst is over, your journey has begun. The trick now is to try and *not* think about your imaginary world (this is also true in a narrative nonfiction piece) even when you're doing laundry and shopping in the supermarket.

10. When you're ready, start work on a draft of scene two. Think about it, get the image clear in your mind, then head for the word processor. When you've printed that scene, work on editing it on the page. When you've finished with that, go back to the word processor and input all the changes you've made on paper to scene one and scene two. Start seeing the flow of scene to scene, of the construction and movement of the story. Your imaginary world is now becoming stronger in your mind, and you are ready to start work on scene three. Keep going this way until you reach the last scene in your narrative. This could take you months to do, but getting a manuscript written is a terrific achievement and one well worth celebrating.

11. Celebration over, start troubleshooting your first draft. This is where the real writing starts. Is there plenty of opposition? Does the story progress well? (Check out chapter twelve for more specific hints as to what to do here.)

12. Now, you think you're ready don't you? You've done a first draft, checked it and virtually done a second draft. Just where *is* that list of agents and editors you met at all those writers conferences and workshops? Sorry, there's more work to do yet. What you have to do now is rewrite the book! You never really know, until you reach the last page, exactly how things will fit together. You need to go back to the beginning of your narrative, now that you've reached the end, and revisit all the changes and ideas that came to you as you wrote, things that deviated from your original synopsis. What you have to do now is try to incorporate all this creativity so it fits seamlessly from start to finish. Take this opportunity to change past events, foreshadow incidents more pointedly, make the end and the beginning meld together in terms of cause and effect.

13. Polish the draft and start reviewing it for style, voice,

grammar, spelling and so forth. (Read and reread Strunk and White's *The Elements of Style!*)

14. Take this wonderful piece of work you've poured your blood sweat and tears into, add the synopsis, which you have polished and adjusted for creative changes as the book has grown and developed, and mail them out. Keep mailing them out until someone says yes.

# WRITING A BOOK PROPOSAL

A book proposal is a description and sample of the structure of a proposed book. Primarily, it's a sales tool. Usually, it's done for a nonfiction book, though there are circumstances where an agent can represent the work of a published novelist in proposal form. However, it's highly unlikely an unpublished, first-time writer will sell a piece of fiction on the strength of a proposal.

That's because nonfiction is essentially about the appeal and marketability of an idea, while fiction also needs some flair and style to its narrative and is much more idiosyncratic in its appeal.

## WRITING THE PROPOSAL

The basic philosophy behind writing a book proposal is two-fold. First, it describes to the editor the book you want to write. Second, it provides the editor with sufficient facts and figures to use as ammunition at an editorial board meeting to convince colleagues in both editorial and sales and marketing that this proposed book is not only a quality piece of work, it will *make money for the publishing company*.

Two of the things writing the proposal can do are help a writer focus and organize a book idea and help a writer become what is expected, from the editor's perspective—that is, an expert in his proposed field.

### The Proposal Structure

Accepted structure for a nonfiction book proposal broadly follows this outline:

- A cover letter.
- Title page.

- A one-paragraph, in-a-nutshell description of the project or idea, that is, the project in a hook format.
- A one- to two-page overview of the project in a dynamic narrative style.
- A market analysis of perhaps half a page, explaining who the audience is for the book and why the book will appeal to them.
- A brief description of competing books, with emphasis on recent commercially successful books in the field (if there are any) and why your book fills a need not currently filled in this field.
- A half-page biography of the writer(s), emphasizing writing experience and any expertise in terms of the proposed subject.
- A table of contents (TOC) that is quite literally a list of chapters and their subheadings (in other words, an at-a-glance description of the book).
- A maximum one-page narrative description of each chapter listed in the TOC.
- A sample chapter or two from the book.

The whole proposal should be twenty to forty pages. Make sure every page of the proposal is bylined in some fashion and, except for the first page, marked with continuous numbering. Always include a self-addressed, stamped envelope (SASE).

## UNIVERSAL APPEAL

To be successful, a proposal should be about an idea that has a universal appeal and could sell ten thousand or more copies. Anything narrower in appeal and subject matter and you are in the realm of small-press books. It's worth remembering that on average it can take perhaps two years from a nonfiction book contract being signed to the book appearing on the shelves, so your book idea must be appealing enough that in two or three years' time, people will still be excited about it.

When submitting to small presses, your proposal should follow the same structure as outlined here, but you need to be certain you have targeted your proposal to the right house and its interests, just as you would if proposing an article to a magazine. You wouldn't send an article suitable for *Playboy* to *Reader's Digest*, for example. Find out what the small press house publishes *before* you submit to it. Ideally, get an editor's name and target a specific editor who will be interested in your project. Probably the best way is to call a publisher and talk to an editorial assistant.

Your proposal should be tightly written, but with a style that has flair and verve. It should offer just enough information in an accessible and hopefully entertaining manner to convince the reader you know your subject and can write well about it. It should also be well organized in a logical progression of ideas and facts and, ideally, reflect the tone and style of the final book.

It's a good idea to do research about competing books as soon as possible, because what you discover may save you a lot of work, disappointment and aggravation if there is no viable market for the book for one reason or another (for instance, someone has just published a book exactly like the one you propose).

Now, another book recently published on your subject may not necessarily be a fatal blow to your book idea, because you may find once you've read the published book that the author treats the subject differently from the way you intend to treat it. It is useful, however, to apprise editors and agents of the fact that you know this other book is in the marketplace and why it won't be a problem for your book idea. If an editor, in ignorance of this other book because you failed to mention it in your proposal, puts forward your idea in an editorial meeting and someone around the table says, "But so-and-so just published a book exactly like this," that editor will have been made to look foolish and ill prepared. Guess whose book she is more than likely *not* going to buy and which author she may not want to work with in the future?

Another good idea is to work on the TOC early on. As you develop the proposal, you'll find you'll continually revise this, but it will provide an excellent overall map to the project while you're working, as well as a guide to its final form when completed.

## THE NONFICTION PROPOSAL

Obviously, you need to pick and choose from the suggestions below because they are inevitably generic. However, following them broadly will give you the kind of information you should be concentrating on putting into your proposal.

As with all sales tools, a book proposal can be broken down into two broad categories: features and benefits.

For example, editors are interested in not only seeing the equivalent of, "This is a high-quality red, four-wheel drive, independent-suspension sport pickup truck," which is a descriptive set of *features* included in the proposal, but also the *benefits* of this truck, for example, "This truck will allow you to not only look good when you take your family to church on Sundays, but will haul all you need to transfer to and from the back pastures the rest of the week."

### The Benefits Section

• **Title Page.** Center your title and the subtitle of the book proposal. Under that add your name and an address and telephone number, voice and fax if you have both (perhaps even an E-mail address). Make yourself easy to reach. Does your answering machine work? Is there a professional message on the machine when an editor or agent does get through? All these things count.

• **The Hook Overview.** The first overview is the hook—a one-sentence or one-paragraph in-a-nutshell description of the book that helps the editor sell the book to colleagues in thirty seconds or less.

• **The Larger Overview.** The second overview is a development of the first. If colleagues say, "This sounds interesting, tell us more," this section provides the editor with broad facts and figures (if applicable) and a general overview of the project. This overview is a much stronger sales tool than your manuscript because it allows you to state not only what the book is about (features), but also why it's important (benefits). How will your book appeal to and help readers? Why does the world need another book on this topic? Answer these questions and you establish your book's identity and commercial worth. Make sure your passion for and interest in your topic shine through. Try to avoid pictures and graphics unless they are extremely well done and relate directly to the proposal's subject.

In general, think about an overview in these terms, although obviously they don't all apply to the same proposal:

1. Why is there a need for this book? What's the problem? What's the hole that needs to be filled? What suffering can you help alleviate in your readers' lives? What information do they lack? What predicament exists in society, or what vacuum needs to be filled? In what new ways can your readers be entertained? State your case as dramatically as you can without being overly sensational. Startle editors and agents from the outset, and make them consider your topic with fresh eyes.

2. How will your book meet this need, fill this hole? Don't answer these questions with hype or rhetoric. Nobody's interested in your opinion of how great this book idea is. Convince potential publishers with solid content summed up in a paragraph or two.

3. How is your book different from others in the field?

4. Why are you the best person to write this book?

5. How long will the manuscript be, and how long will it take you to write it?

6. Close your overview with something that sums up the benefits or merits of the book, reminding the reader of the book's importance.

7. Try and do all this in no more than four double-spaced pages, and ideally two.

• **Market Analysis.** In this section, you need to explain who the audience is for your book; that is, who's going to go into a store and plunk down six dollars for a paperback (or thirteen dollars for a trade paperback or twenty-two dollars for a hardcover) version of your book. What evidence can you offer that your assessment is accurate? Use facts and figures you have researched. How many people belong to organizations or subscribe to magazines that deal with this topic? What other books out there have proven there is a successful and eager audience for your proposed book? Why will these people still be interested in reading about your topic in two years' time, or five years' time (what publishers call a book's backlist life). Give statistics about groups who may be interested in buying copies of the book. Go online, and haunt the library. You have to be factual and realistic. It won't help to be sloppy or overly generalized in your assessment. If you have experience or knowledge in selling, marketing or promoting, mention that. Do you have a seminar you take around from place to place? Do you lecture to groups of people regularly? What can you do to translate your experiences into book sales? A strong marketing plan accompanying a book proposal will go a long way in helping to sell the proposal. Are you a member of organizations who will help publicize your book and, ideally, buy lots of copies? Could you help sell bulk quantities of your book to organizations who might want to give them away as gifts to members? Do you have a connection to well-known people who might endorse your book and help increase book sales that way?

- **Competing Books.** What we mean here is a list of a half dozen or so of the most successful and most recent books published in the field you propose to write about. Nothing breeds success like success, particularly if you have a new take on a successful idea. In your comments about the books, include title, author, year of publication, publisher, a one- or two-sentence description and a statement pointing out the difference between your book and the published book. Every competing book gives you an opportunity to make a new point about your book idea, so take advantage of the opportunity. Again, use the library and the Internet for your research.

Browse the bookstores in your area; befriend bookstore owners; chat with book people in general. If there is nothing in the
field to compare with your book, make certain you convince
editors and agents there really is a market for the book, and
you're just the first person to have spotted a hole and decided
to fill it.

## The Features Section

• **Table of Contents.** Here you explain how the book will
be organized and what it will say. The simple table of contents
will list the number of chapters you intend to have in your
book and what the subtitle of each chapter will be (for example, Chapter 1: Joe Is Born; Chapter 2: Joe Goes to School;
Chapter 3: Joe Discovers Baseball for the First Time, etc.). The
TOC provides an at-a-glance guide to the book's content and
organization, and, through your subtitling, perhaps a glimpse
of the wit or seriousness you intend to bring to the project.
At least 75 percent of a book proposal's success lies in its
organization. You may have a great idea, but if you present it
poorly, it shows not only a poor writing ability, but also poor
thought processes, and in nonfiction a logical exploration of
an idea and an easily graspable progression of thought is more
or less what you are offering, beyond the originality of the
idea in question. Agents and editors look for books that are
logical, well written and organized according to a plan that is
obvious and accessible to your readers. For example, a client
of mine proposed a book about parent activism in educational
reform by profiling a dozen or so schools around the country
that have been turned around by parent activism. In the end,
however, we decided a better structure was to identify a dozen
or so things parents could do, from starting a new school and
hiring teachers to improving a school's looks, and then use
the examples of the schools to show how some problems
were solved. The reader was more immediately interested in
a book of problems and solutions than in profiles of success
stories.

• **Chapter-by-Chapter Descriptions.** Now that you've

nailed down the overall structure of your book, write a half-page to one-page description of what you plan to cover in each chapter. The key here, as throughout the proposal, is your ability to write succinctly, yet dynamically, about your subject. In general, state your premise and then explain how you will develop it. Make sure that, as in your overview, your passion and interest for your subject come through. An effective second-person voice can work here: "Have you ever thought about what life would be like without access to water? Your life, and the lives of those around you would be vastly different. . . . "

• **Sample Chapters.** This is self-explanatory. A nonfiction book needs a mixture of narrative, emotion, and logic to work well. So it doesn't matter what chapters you include, but you should aim at about fifteen to twenty pages. No more than two chapters needs to be included. If you use partial chapters, make sure everyone knows these are not the complete versions of the chapters.

• **Author Biography.** Nowadays you have to be an expert, or a professional writer who is working in collaboration with one or more experts, to get a nonfiction book successfully published. You have to be an expert because you will be competing with others who are experts who have published books in this field, even if their books aren't very good. So establish you credibility both as a writer and as an expert in the topic you are proposing. That may mean writing articles on your proposed subject and getting them published in magazines before you start querying editors and agents with your book idea. Try and write your bio in third person, rather than first person, unless you have a life experience that makes your view particularly valid.

• **The Cover Letter.** This should be brief and warm and probably contain the hook. It should include your address and phone numbers and other relevant information, such as you're a prize-winning writer, a member of this or that group, an expert in the topic you propose, referred by a writer or agent, whatever. Mention the book's title and what kind of book it is, then let the proposal do the rest of the work.

## THE FICTION PROPOSAL

The fiction proposal is a simpler document. In nonfiction, you're selling an idea, well organized and well presented. In fiction, you need to reassure an editor that an idea for a novel can be expanded successfully to a book-length manuscript, usually three to four hundred pages in length, double-spaced. So editors tend to want to see the whole thing rather than trust to luck.

If you have not published fiction before, unless you are writing fiction based on your widely recognized field of expertise (for example, you're a NASA astronaut writing a science fiction thriller based on your experiences), editors are not likely to take a chance on an unfinished manuscript. They don't really need to, because there are so many accomplished writers out there, eager to get published, who already have finished manuscripts to choose from.

Most fiction proposals that succeed in getting an author published come from experienced writers an editor knows can provide a well-written finished manuscript. The editor is concerned not with, "Can he write a good novel?" but with, "Is this a good idea for a novel that we can successfully sell to the public?"

The fiction proposal will once again provide the hook and a brief overview. It will also include a synopsis of the story, detailing, in broad narrative strokes, the beginning, middle and end of your story over the shoulder of the main character(s). It should include a bio of the author, emphasizing writing experience and publications, and the *first* thirty to fifty pages of the book. If the first few chapters aren't the best in the book and don't hook the reader, it doesn't matter how brilliant the rest of the book is, the reader will never get to it. If a writer of fiction chooses to send chapters other than the first chapters to an editor, the suggestion is that the first chapters need work and, consequently, the book is not ready for submission.

If the book is part of a series of books, it's a good idea to include a half-page or one-page description of a couple of further titles in the series, as well as a brief series overview.

Propose ideas one at a time.

Don't inundate an editor or agent with a shopping list of ideas at one time on the basis of, "If you don't like this, then try that." It's unprofessional and shows a lack of commitment and passion to the project.

## SAMPLE PROPOSAL

What follows is a sample nonfiction proposal. It was originally submitted by my client Christine Goff and is an excellent example of the kind of nonfiction proposal structure I've been discussing in this chapter. Note that the sample chapters are not included here but would be included with the actual proposal.

# DYSLEXIA: The Road to Triumph

### *A True-Life Experience and Parent-Friendly Guide to Raising a Child With Dyslexia*

**by
Christine Goff**

(Address and telephone number supplied here)

## OVERVIEW

Every year in the United States approximately 96,000 students are diagnosed with dyslexia, a specific learning disability characterized by problems in processing oral or written language. In fact, of the nearly 2.25 million students receiving special education services through the U.S. school system, researchers estimate nearly 1.8 million of those children suffer from dyslexia.

How many more students slip through the cracks, undiagnosed or deemed ineligible for services? The National Institutes of Health estimate as many as 15 percent of American students may be classified as dyslexic, while studies from Yale University indicate that reading difficulties affect 1 in 5 individuals. That's 20 percent of the overall population. With approximately 15 million school-aged children, the numbers indicate a staggering 2.25 to 3 million students may actually be suffering from dyslexia.

And suffering is the correct word. The effects on the child and the family are incalculable, but they don't have to be demoralizing. *Dyslexia: The Road to Triumph* will blend the ironic, painful and humorous sides of one family's struggle to overcome dyslexia with valuable steps for negotiating the potholes along the way. Meant to entertain and inspire, the book's focus is to provide information parents need to empower the choices they will make raising a child with dyslexia.

My experience raising a child with dyslexia showed me the need for a comprehensive, step-by-step guide to raising a child with reading disabilities. To that end, I have detailed the following parent-friendly steps:

1. *Define the problem.* Recognizing that your child has a problem is only the beginning. A variety of things could be causing your child's difficulty, but once you've eliminated the

obvious, it's time to dig deeper.

II. *Find the experts.* Educators, therapists, psychologists and doctors all have differing opinions on how to diagnose and prescribe treatment—ranging from placating advice to aggressive intervention. Finding someone whose opinion you trust can be a challenge in and of itself; finding the proper testing can be nearly impossible.

III. *Ask questions.* Once you find the experts, you need to know what questions to ask. Sometimes the answers are scary, but more often they help you understand what you can do to help your child triumph over his or her disability.

IV. *Deal with the powers that be.* Once you've determined the problem and the course of treatment, you'll need to enlist the help of family and the school. While you should be able to count on family, the schools are not always so accommodating. To that end you need to know the laws, and what you can and cannot expect from your school system.

V. *Check out other methods of remediation.* While most schools choose traditional ways of dealing with dyslexia, there are a variety of other methods and things you can try that may, or may not, help your child. There are special libraries, exercises, vitamins and treatments available, as well as private schools that specialize in working with children with "special needs." And there are psychological issues that go along with being diagnosed "dyslexic."

Finally, *Dyslexia: The Road to Triumph* would not be complete without success stories and appendixes of helpful resources.

In addition to my daughter's triumphs, there are a number of well-known individuals who suffer from reading disabilities—

Albert Einstein, Whoopi Goldberg, John Travolta, Charles Schwab, Nelson Rockefeller, John Irving, Tom Cruise, Stephen Cannell—all of whom have found success in spite of being dyslexic. Mr. Cannell (the best-selling author of three novels and the creator/cocreator of over forty television shows, including *The Rockford Files*, *The A-Team*, *Wiseguy* and *Silk Stalkings*) spoke with me recently regarding his dyslexia and offered advice to my daughter on coping with her disability. I am willing to approach Mr. Cannell to write a foreword for *Dyslexia: The Road to Triumph*.

Appendixes will include lists of support organizations, treatment centers, suggested reading for parents, recommended reading books for children with dyslexia and computer software publishers with programs designed to help children with reading disabilities.

It takes parents and educators who understand the issues and have the tools to address the problems facing children with dyslexia. Unlike other books on the subject, *Dyslexia: The Road to Triumph* does not attempt to explain learning disabilities, only to define what's at stake for the child who has trouble with written and oral language and provide a plan for dealing with the primary learning disability in America—dyslexia.

## MARKET ANALYSIS

*Dyslexia: The Road to Triumph* could not be more timely. Dyslexia is the number one cause of learning difficulties in the United States. While dyslexia is sometimes construed as a catchall phrase for learning disabilities, recent research confirming a genetic link with reading difficulties has sparked new interest in treatments for the disorder. More and more experts are acknowledging that dyslexia results from differences in the brain, and thus that dyslexics learn differently from other children. (A case in point: Psychologists at the University of Colorado have developed a computer program and learning approach that, combined with early detection, can teach the dyslexic new ways of learning.)

In today's computer age, mastery of the written and oral language is becoming more and more mandatory. Children are expected to excel at earlier ages. When combined with the rise in literacy programs, the increasing number of American students suffering from learning disabilities, and the inability of our school systems to handle the numbers in the classroom, the need for a book that empowers parents to help their child with dyslexia succeed clearly emerges.

## APPROACH

*Dyslexia: The Road to Triumph* will be a 60,000- to 70,000-word book targeted to parents raising a child with dyslexia. Unlike other books on the subject, *Dyslexia* will provide personal anecdotes along with simple, easy-to-understand information on raising a child with a reading disability. It will be written in an informal, friendly manner and begin with the first-person accounting of our discovery that our daughter had a reading disability. Subsequent chapters will weave the ongoing process of that discovery with concrete steps a parent can take to avoid the potholes of the journey through the diagnosis, treatment, battles and victories.

In addition to walking the reader through the process from the moment of discovery, *Dyslexia* offers explanations of the testing process and laws designed to protect the student and lists of useful contacts and reading material. At the end of the book, readers will find a useful list of some of the reading books available for the dyslexic child, broken down by reading level and content. While by no means a comprehensive list, it serves as a starting point for the parents desperate to find appropriate reading books for their child.

Through example and encouragement, *Dyslexia* will offer parents a variety of strategies for helping their child cope with dyslexia. An accessible and practical book, *Dyslexia* will give readers a process to work through their problem and set their child on the road to triumph.

## THE COMPETITION

Most existing books on the market approach the subject from a therapist's or educator's point of view. There is little offered in layman's terms to help parents better understand their role in remediation of their child's dyslexia, and what is offered is mostly out-of-date.

*Something's Not Right*, by Nancy Lelewer (VanderWyk & Burnham, 1994), is a first-person, autobiographical account of one learning-disabled mother's experience raising two children with learning disabilities. Little is offered in the way of resources or references, though parent's will find the story comforting.

*LD and Your Child*, by Lawrence J. Greene (Fawcett, 1987), offers primary case studies on various types of learning disabilities. Written in a very academic tone, this book offers limited use to the parent.

*Help Me to Help My Child*, by Jill Bloom (Little, Brown & Co., 1990), is written in question and answer format and gives a general overview of learning disabilities. While there are several good directories in the back, the text is written in high language with little white space, making for tedious reading.

*The Misunderstood Child*, by Larry B. Silver. (McGraw-Hill, 1984), opens with a case study. This book describes learning disabilities in general from a psychiatrist's perspective. A strong believer in traditional remediation, Dr. Silver sends out a gloomy tone on the prognosis of raising a learning-disabled child.

The most helpful book I could find was *Parenting a Child With a Learning Disability*, by Cheryl Gerson Tuttle and Penny Paquette (Lowell House, 1993). Tuttle and Paquette give a good overall view of learning disabilities. They define what it means to have a learning disability, describe the self-esteem issues, home life, adolescence, the various types of learning disabilities, testing and evaluation procedures, the laws and provide lists of support organizations and state-by-state contacts. While extremely thorough, Tuttle and Paquette's treatment of all learning disabilities makes it extremely difficult to sift out the information offered about dyslexia.

Other books available on dyslexia and reading disabilities are either sold by a specific treatment center or organization, specifically written for educators or therapists, exceedingly expensive or self-published.

## THE AUTHOR

Christine Goff is the mother of a daughter diagnosed with dyslexia, two daughters who are being watched closely for signs of reading difficulties and three grown stepchildren, one of whom showed signs of dyslexia while growing up (though she was never officially diagnosed). A freelance writer, Goff has written columns and articles for local and regional newspapers and magazines beginning in 1985, and published a first-person essay on parental competition in *Mothers Today* magazine, a national publication. She has been a part-time editor for Chockstone Press, a nonfiction publisher specializing in rock and ice climbing guides, and currently edits *Deadlines*, the newsletter of the Rocky Mountain Chapter of Mystery Writers of America, and *The Rocky Mountain Writer*, newsletter of The Rocky Mountain Fiction Writers.

Her success in seeing one daughter through being labeled a "lazy student" and "slow learner" to acceptance at a prestigious private school known for it's gifted students is a testament to her understanding of the process of learning to cope with dyslexia, of finding the way to triumph.

# TABLE OF CONTENTS

Dedication

Acknowledgments

Table of Contents

Foreword

Introduction

**Step I.   Define the Problem**
She's Slow!
Reactions
The Elimination Process

**Step II.  Find the Experts**
What the Schools Should Do!
Too Much Advice
Meeting Meredith

**Step III. Ask Questions**
The Test
The Diagnosis
What is Dyslexia?
Meredith's Solution

**Step IV. Deal with the Powers That Be**
Friends, Family and The Schools
The Law
The Stigma

**Step V.  Check Out Other Methods of Remediation**
Private vs. Public School

# CHAPTER OUTLINE

Introduction
A short overview of dyslexia and the numbers of children affected by the learning disability.

## Step I: Define the Problem

Epigraph

Chapter 1: She's Slow!
This chapter recounts the day the author was told her daughter, Mardee, had a reading problem. (See sample chapters.)

Chapter 2: Reactions
How you react to the news that your child is struggling with reading affects the way your child's teacher reacts, the way friends and family perceive the problem and how your child feels about himself or herself. Underreact and the teacher thinks you're an uncaring parent. Overreact and the teacher becomes defensive and uncooperative.
Following a recap of the author's experience, which included reopening the lines of communication with Mardee's teacher, the remaining chapter covers the following:

1. The warning signs of a reading disability. This will help keep readers from being caught unaware.
2. Ways to approach your child's teacher so that he or she becomes an ally and not your enemy.
3. Ways to approach the school administrator should the teacher be uncooperative or less concerned than you are.

Chapter 3: The Elimination Process

Once it's discovered that your child has a reading problem, you need to determine the reason. Reading difficulties result from a variety of causes.

The author recounts the experience of putting Mardee through the battery of exams required to eliminate the "easy" answers.

1. The doctor visit. There are any number of ailments that can cause your child to be distracted from learning to read—stomachaches, headaches, allergies.

2. The ophthalmologist visit. Whether or not your child can see the blackboard or the words on the page can be a big factor in learning to read. A simple eye test and prescription glasses may solve the problem.

3. The audiology exam. Hearing also plays a factor in learning to read. In addition to not knowing what's going on in the classroom, the child who can't hear may suffer from imbalances that make it difficult to learn.

4. The psychological exam. Last, as with almost everything else, when the doctors and specialists find nothing else wrong, the cause is often attributed to psychological difficulties. Most schools, teachers and doctors will recommend having the child seen by a "specialist." And, though it adds to your child's feeling that something is wrong with him or her, it doesn't hurt to rule out the psychological factor.

### Step II: Find the Experts

Epigraph

Chapter 4: What Schools Should Do!

Once the preliminary round of examinations is complete, you must go back to the schools. At this point your teacher should recommend your child be "tested." However, as the author's experience illustrates, what should happen and what does happen are often different things.

This chapter contains a brief overview of a school's responsibility, with reference to Chapter 12: The Law. One reason schools don't always adhere to the requirements is money. Another is the overwhelming number of children who require help.

Chapter 5: Too Much Advice

At this stage, you are often overwhelmed by the difficulties facing your child. What do we do now? you wonder. How can you help your child to "catch up," as junior falls farther and farther behind.

As the author relates, the advice offered is often thoughtless, and hurtful. In this chapter are suggestions for how to handle the well-meaning, misinformed and downright mean individuals who approach you with solutions.

Chapter 6: Meeting Meredith

It took a roundabout way to find help for Mardee, a process you don't have to experience when seeking help for your child. This chapter includes suggestions on finding the experts.

1. Check the phone book. Most of the large cities have associations or organizations for the learning disabled. They can steer you in the right direction.

2. Contact one of the national support organizations (Appendix A). They should have lists of doctors and therapists in your area

or suggestions on finding someone who specializes in learning or reading disabilities.

3. Contact one of the treatment centers specializing in reading difficulties (Appendix B). While they have their own treatment plans, they can steer you in a variety of directions.

4. Call your local children's hospital, the method the author used when all else failed.

### Step III: Ask Questions

Epigraph

Chapter 7: The Test

The author contacted a friend, who put her in touch with a therapist at Children's Hospital in Denver, Colorado. Meredith, a member of the nationally renowned M.O.R.E. team, submitted Mardee to another battery of exams, including speech and audio evaluations and a variety of intelligence tests.

This chapter includes a list of the tests, an overview of the most popularly used and a brief summary of the results.

Chapter 8: The Diagnosis

It's difficult for parents and child alike when the diagnosis of dyslexia is confirmed. Dyslexia is a learning disability that never goes away. You can learn to deal with it, cope with it, succeed with it, but you can't ever get rid of it. Parents and child experience a period of grief.

We went through a period of denial, convinced that with the right treatment, Mardee's dyslexia would go away. Convinced that things would suddenly "click in," as Mardee's teacher had suggested.

Mardee felt very angry, then very sad. She wanted to know why she couldn't just be "like everybody else."

The grieving process can leave you feeling very stupid. After all, your child isn't dying. He or she can have a normal life, a great career, a wonderful marriage. This chapter offers suggestions on how to deal with the diagnosis and then move on.

Chapter 9: What is Dyslexia?

This chapter gives a history of dyslexia from the first recognition of the disorder alexia by English physicians (Morgan and Kerr in 1896-97) and the work of Dr. Samuel Orton and Anna Gillingham to the recent discovery of a genetic link. In addition, the chapter contains an explanation of how dyslexia affects a child's learning and the possible causes, along with a profile of the typical dyslexic: a child whose reading skills are below grade level, but whose intelligence measures in the high-average to above-average range. Children with dyslexia are often extremely bright and are usually exceptionally creative.

Chapter 10: Meredith's Solution

When Meredith gave the treatment recommendation and prognosis, the author knew the family would have trouble meeting the financial expense of paying a therapist. However, proceeding with remediation seemed the only logical choice. To her surprise, financial aid was available to help alleviate the burden.

This chapter outlines the prognosis of a child with dyslexia as well as the three general categories of treatment and ways to help pay for the treatment:

1. The developmental approach. This is sometimes referred to as the "more of the same" approach. Teachers and parents often

feel that the methods that have been previously used to teach the child are adequate and that the child just needs extra time and attention to "get it." Often the children are placed in small-group or tutorial sessions.

2. The corrective reading method also uses small-group session, but emphasis is placed on the child's assets and interests. Those using this method hope to encourage children to rely on their own special abilities to overcome their difficulties.

3. Remediation was developed primarily to address the shortcomings of the first two methods. Small groups or one-on-one tutoring is employed, where a therapist recognizes a child's assets but teaches toward correcting the student's deficiencies. Multisensory techniques are used, as well as structured repetition.

## Step IV: Deal With the Powers That Be

Epigraph

Chapter 11: Friends, Family and the School

Then comes the time for explaining the facts to family, friends and school. You need to enlist aid in helping with the remediation process. Of course, you shouldn't expect everyone to be helpful.

Our experience in dealing with the schools demonstrates how difficult it can sometimes be. The school personnel's reaction in Mardee's case was to "retest" her using their tests and their tester. The only problem was, Mardee had to explain to the test administrator *how* to give the test. Needless to say, the results came out dramatically different from the results at Children's Hospital.

Chapter 12: The Law

This chapter deals with what you can, by law, insist your school do for your child.

Had we known what we could have "demanded," we might have saved ourselves a lot of money and headaches in the process of diagnosing Mardee's dyslexia. There are a number of federal laws that protect children with disabilities: Public Law 94-142—Education for Handicapped Children Act, Section 504 of the Rehabilitation Act of 1973; FERPA—Family Educational Rights and Privacy Act; and Public Law 99-457. In addition, there are state laws that protect your child's rights and can assist you in getting an official "staffing" for your child.

Knowing the laws can help you and your child get the help you need, but there is a downside.

Chapter 13: The Stigma

Having your child "staffed" often means including the child in the special education classes. While this can sometimes be a benefit, most times it places a stigma on your child that may be difficult to live with.

Mardee was extremely embarrassed about her disability and wanted to hide her problems. Often this is the case. At the age most children are diagnosed with dyslexia, they just want to be like everyone else. They want to fit in, be the same. This is not an age where individualism counts.

But children with dyslexia are different. They think differently, process differently, learn differently. In a society in which the school system is set up to encourage those children who are reading and writing above the norm, children with dyslexia can feel like total misfits. In a classroom where children are reading chapter books, children with dyslexia are barely able to decipher what others deem as "baby books."

## Step V: Check Out Other Methods of Remediation

Epigraph

Chapter 14: Private vs. Public Schools

It was at this time the author chose to move her daughter to a private school. The classroom size was smaller, more conducive to the one-on-one reading aid Mardee needed. In addition, the teachers were better able to accommodate Mardee's "special needs": grading homework papers for content only rather than marking her down for spelling errors, allowing her to present her work through oral or photographic reports, affording her opportunities to learn in hands-on projects.

There are a number of private schools designed to teach children with dyslexia and/or learning disabilities. Denver Academy in Denver, Colorado, is one such school. Its curriculum is designed for the college-bound student. Its population is made up of entirely learning-disabled children.

This chapter includes addresses and phone numbers for organizations you can contact to help locate private schools in your area. Many are able to offer financial assistance to students who apply in a timely fashion.

Chapter 15: Special Treatments

In addition to the typical types of remediation, there are a number of other therapies available. Many are regarded as "flaky" by the traditionalists, but some have merit.

Mardee was progressing slowly under Meredith's tutoring. As time went on, Mardee became more and more frustrated with the slow progress and we decided to "experiment" with several other techniques (while continuing the more traditional remediation). This chapter relates some of those experiences and details the alternative treatments available, including the following:

1. Color Therapy
2. Eye Therapy
3. Ear Treatments
4. Brain Gym
5. Lindamood-Bell Therapy
6. Holistic Vitamin Therapy

(See sample chapters.)

Chapter 16: Special Resources

In addition to alternative therapy, there are special resources available for the children with dyslexia. There are special programs they can participate in and special tools for them to use. One is the Talking Book Library System for the Blind and Reading Disabled. Books on tape, tape recorders and free mail service are provided by these special libraries, opening the world of reading to your child.

Mardee was very discouraged at not being able to decode information at a level she was capable of comprehending. Once we connected with the Colorado Talking Book Library, she was able to "read" books that her peers were reading, allowing her to discuss literature and opening doors that had been slammed shut before.

Chapter 17: The Status Quo

Things are changing rapidly in the research and treatment of dyslexia. Theories abound about early diagnosis and intervention versus waiting until the problem rears its head at age seven or eight; the difference in the brain of the child with dyslexia versus the child without dyslexia; and the correlation with other learning disabilities.

Researchers are creating and testing new computer programs for use in the schools for children with dyslexia. For instance, the University of Colorado has been testing a computer program in the Boulder, Colorado, school system that teaches children with dyslexia new ways of learning to read.

Organizations such as the Mystery Writers of America (MWA) are recognizing the need for "high-content, easy vocabulary" books for children and adults who struggle to read. Members of MWA are working with NTC/Contemporary Publishing Company, a leading publisher of adult education materials, to develop a series of mysteries, to be released in 1998, for older students and adults with limited reading skills.

This chapter highlights some of the ongoing research and projects that aid parents and educators in the remediation process.

Epigraph

Success Stories

There are a large number of very successful people with dyslexia, including Whoopi Goldberg, John Travolta, Charles Schwab, Nelson Rockefeller, John Irving, Tom Cruise and Stephen Cannell. It's even been said Albert Einstein and Thomas Edison suffered from dyslexia.

This chapter relates Mardee's success in coping with her disability, as well as recounting the success stories of other more well-known individuals with dyslexia.

Appendix A

A list of support organizations, such as The Learning Disabilities Association of America, Orton Dyslexia Society, Dyslexia Association of America and the National Center for Learning Disabilities.

Appendix B

A list of treatment centers, such as APSL-Derived Programs, Lindamood-Bell Learning Centers, Orton Dyslexia Society Learning Centers and the Herman Method Institute.

Appendix C

A recommended reading list for parents.

Appendix D

A list of recommended reading books for dyslexic children, broken down by ability level and content level.

Appendix E

A list of computer software publishers that carry programs of use in working with a dyslexic child.

# INDEX